COCO

A BIOGRAPHY

Descent from Parnassus   (Cresset Press)

Remember Greece   (Hodder & Stoughton)

The Traveller's Journey is Done   (Hodder & Stoughton)

Films Since 1939   (Longmans)

MANLY POODLES have beards and whiskers. Coco, sent to the barber for a beard-trim, surprised his owners by coming home clean-shaven

DILYS POWELL

COCO

A BIOGRAPHY

'Prattling away about poodle dogs in
the age of atom bomb . . .'

EXASPERATED CORRESPONDENT

LONDON
HODDER & STOUGHTON

First published 1952

PRINTED IN GREAT BRITAIN FOR
HODDER & STOUGHTON LTD, LONDON BY
W. S. COWELL LTD, IPSWICH

ILLUSTRATIONS

v

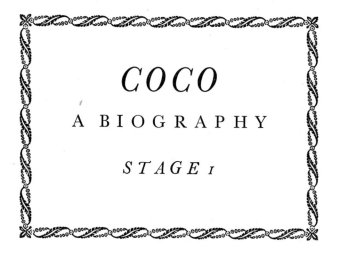

COCO

A BIOGRAPHY

STAGE 1

I

IT IS COMMONLY the misfortune of the bio-
grapher to know his subject at long range only,
through a cloud of years and documents. I can claim
at least one title to write this biography: that I knew
its subject in his infancy. Our first meeting took place
when he was two months old.

I was, to tell the truth, not altogether eager for the
encounter. A passion for dogs is one of the few I can
curb. Years ago, a novice journalist with more confidence than judgement, I innocently took a furnished
attic in a quarter of London where journalism is not
the profession expected of solitary young women.
The ground floor was a bakery. The intervening
floors were occupied by families of a respectability on
which the members daily congratulated themselves,
and my presence was clearly regarded as a blot on
the purity of the house. The third floor included
among its tenants a repulsive little terrier with

3

inflexible bow legs who rushed at me, barking with moral fervour, every time I passed. One day he went lame, and his owners accused me of kicking him. A week or two later I accidently learned that the creature was rheumatic and periodically fell to hobbling, a fact of which nobody in the house had thought proper to inform me. Remorse I have long thought to be, like revenge, sterile and a waste of time. But I confess that I sometimes give way to regret for the sins I have not committed but omitted, and high in the list is my regret that I never kicked that dog.

My early experience of this zealot, combined with a stay of some years in Greece, where every shepherd's dog used to be trained, apparently, to kill at sight, had put me against the friend of man, and though later acquaintances, of whom I shall presently find something to say, had softened my mood, I was still inclined to look on most dogs simply as animals which ought to be fitted with silencers. In any case I was reluctant to take on a new pet. Indolent, a postponer, always ready to convince myself that I ought to ring up thingumabob before beginning to write an article, I had trouble enough as it was in making myself work. For heaven's sake, I thought, let's not make things harder than they are: no worrying about taking Towser for a run.

And there was the cat to consider. For thirteen years a Siamese cat had shared my life. He had been good enough during the war to sanction my marriage; for special circumstances had recommended my husband to him; as a matter of fact Leonard had given me my cat, a first incomparable present, in the Hitler-ridden winter of 1936. My wedding thus brought no stranger into the house. But the cat, named Periander after the tyrant of Corinth, and familiarly called Perry, had never been tolerant of rivals with his own number of legs. Once the Campbell Dixons, unwilling to leave their kitten in an empty flat during the air raids, had brought the tiny thing to dinner with them. Perry spent the evening sitting on top of the books on the highest shelf, growling, and when I went to lift him down reminded me of the respect he was owed by biting me in the right forearm. Occasionally a neighbour's pet would stray in through an open window; if we failed to hear the sounds of battle we still had the evidence of our eyes; to the treads of the stairs clung tufts of tabby or black fur, mixed I admit with wisps of silky beige. And I remembered a regrettable incident in the blitz when my daily maid, bombed out, took refuge with me and brought her cat, a massive black-and-white neuter. Perry despised the sheep-like creature with the slow movements and the bat-squeak. He waited his chance; then one morning with elaborate caution he sneaked up behind the visitor and bit him smartly in the rear. I can still hear the eunuch's dreadful womanish scream.

All the same Perry had never been afraid of dogs, and now that he was growing old he would, Leonard argued, probably ignore altogether so foolish a thing as a puppy. It was true that in the last year or two he had withdrawn a little from society. Though he still now and then flung his arms round my neck or Leonard's, he had lost the old rapture in which he would delicately tweak one's nose with his teeth. He no longer slept under our eiderdown or crept up in the dawn, brushed our cheeks with the soft back of a careful paw, and asked to be invited between the sheets. He preferred to lie alone at night in the warm, silent kitchen; the days he dreamed away, and he scarcely bothered to chatter at the sparrows which hopped in the yard. Perhaps Leonard was right. Perhaps Perry at thirteen years old really was past jealousy. I could not feel sure. I was afraid of hurting the feelings of my old favourite; or possibly I was once more giving way to my weakness for postponement. At any rate left to myself I should have done nothing. Had Leonard not taken matters into his own hands I should never have met our dog, and this biography would never have been written.

It had all started years ago when one morning we saw bouncing down our street a large chocolate-coloured bundle of astrakhan. What can it be? we asked; for in those days the poodle, and particularly the unshaven poodle, was not everybody's dog. Our question answered, we began to look out for poodles; and suddenly they were everywhere: miniature and full-size, black, white, brown and grey. The mixture of beautiful and absurd in the breed entranced us; here, we felt, was the exquisite oddity, the Siamese of the dog world. We must, said Leonard, have a poodle. But in the life of a journalist, and especially of a couple of journalists, plans are made to be set aside. A dozen chances intervene—the new piece of work, the trip to somewhere or other, the broadcasts, the lectures, the committees, the good causes. Time roared by. The war ended, Governments fell, new wars impended, and Leonard was still saying that we must have a poodle.

At last, in one of those flashes of decision born of years of rumbling, he took action. A poodle resident in Campden Hill had recently littered; a friend, learning from a chance meeting with her owner that the puppies were for sale, rang up to tell us. When I came home that night I found that we were committed to buying a poodle.

I must make it clear that neither of us knew anything about choosing a puppy. Leonard's family had owned dogs but, notoriously tender-hearted, had usually out of kindness and affection taken the animals in full-grown. In my home there had not been a dog since my childhood. I had no ideas on training a puppy beyond a suspicion that the creature frequently ran away and must be recaptured. I had never in my life fed a dog. As for the proper shape of head, shade of nose, size of ears, texture of coat, arrangement of teeth and set-on of tail, I was as ignorant as I am of atomic physics.

Even on the subject of colour I had no views. What do you think, I asked Leonard before, heavy with the responsibility, I set off to choose a poodle, what colour would you like? Whichever you like, he said. Pressed, he added that he rather liked apricot. Apricot? I asked. Leonard had already seen the puppies; he described the mother and a grown-up son from an earlier litter leaping in powerful play while on the floor beneath them, looking up serenely amidst the thunder of pads, stood a fawn-coloured infant. I believe that was an apricot, he said; but choose what you like; choose the one which chooses you.

All through my visit I struggled to make a choice. The poodle nursery, I found, was an outhouse at the end of a walled courtyard; the family lived immured in warmth and faint canine smells. For the mother, perhaps, the sensuous, inactive hours were beginning after eight weeks to lose their charm. At any rate when the door was opened she disengaged herself from the Laocoon-mass of legs and noses inside, rushed across the yard and jumped in through the dining-room window. Seven puppies gambolled behind her and through the door. The eighth hesitated, reluctant to risk the four-inch drop from the threshold of the shed; at last he too lurched out and joined the romp indoors. Yes, said the owner, he's the one your husband noticed. Is that an apricot? I asked. He's apricot-coloured now, said the owner, but poodles have a tendency to grow lighter. His mother is a blue, but she was black as a puppy; he'll probably be what's called a cream. He was also, I learned, the runt of the litter. Nature's wasteful economy had provided one puppy too many; beaten in the battle to suck from his mother, he had been fed by hand.

In the kitchen the mother ate her biscuits while the owner cooked a meal for the family: a kind of gruel made of tinned baby-milk, fresh milk and semolina. The puppies scampered through the other rooms: fawn puppies, grey, black, brown. At the slightest gesture they flew one and all to paw my skirt. I was in a twitch of indecision. Impossible for me to say, adopting the standards of the Poodle Club, this muzzle is long but not snipey, or these hocks are well let down. All hocks looked alike to me, and I had to choose by liking, not judgement. I put off the moment of selection. How often are they fed? I asked. Can they be trained to stay alone in the house? At what age should they be inoculated against distemper? And yet had I been perceptive enough I should have known that the choice was already made. Already a muzzle, not at all snipey, was thrusting more resolutely than the rest at my hand. Already a paw, or to speak correctly the promise of a tight foot, knuckled up, was scratching monotonously for attention. I realize now that from the very start a puppy had chosen me.

When I went out to find a taxi the mother came with me for the ride. A finger across the nose, I was instructed, meant: don't cross the road now, wait till I tell you. To my relief it worked, and as we stood together on the curb in Notting Hill Gate I suddenly felt what I can describe only as doggy. In fact when the wife of a colleague, happening to pass by, stopped to felicitate me on my beautiful poodle I found myself falsely simpering. A few minutes later I was driving home through the November dusk. On my lap, triumphantly beaming, sat a little fawn-coloured puppy with a broad head, a foreshortened muzzle, long silky ears and an enormous milk chocolate nose. He was, I need hardly say, the runt of the litter; and he bore, so far as I could see, no resemblance of any kind to a poodle.

2

'*DO NOT SHUT YOUR PUPPY* out of the family councils', says an authority on poodles. It would have been impossible to shut our puppy out of anything, for from the moment of his arrival he insisted on accompanying us everywhere, even at the expense of modesty. No matter how fast asleep, he woke at our least withdrawal. We would slip through the door, steal into the next room, creep downstairs with, as we thought, the silence of a butterfly. This time, we said, we have escaped him, but when we looked round there he was, waddling devotedly at our heels. He follows us round, we told one another delightedly, like a dog.

Clearly one of our first duties was to name this solid shadow. We considered his parentage. His mother's drawing-room name was Mistinguette Noire; his father's Frenches Blue Peter. Behind them stretched a line of titles in which the Piperscroft and

Vulcan strains appeared and reappeared: Ch. Vulcan Champagne Pommery, Ch. Quality of Piperscroft, and still farther away such verbal rock-work as Coppertop of Astolat, Berkham Apollo, Nunsoe d'Amour and Chilham Mingo. There was even an American great-great-grandfather, U.S.A. Ch. Blackeen Durante of Gilltown. But though our protégé's nose was on the Durante scale, it was not to his American connections that we found ourselves looking for a name.

Many people say that the poodle is a sporting Russian who trotted westward. The authorities differ about the date of his going, but one school of thought maintains that he arrived in France, as might be expected of a dog with so pacific a temper, a little late for the Revolution. The Germans, too, claim him. Certainly his name is German: Pudel, a splasher, a water-dog. But in our Francophil family we like to think of him as French: our dog, we say, is a French poodle; and it was a French name which first came to mind.

A friend of mine was once travelling by train in France with a little white woolly dog. It was a hot journey, the compartment was full, and the ticket-collector was disagreeable; he clipped each ticket in sour silence and handed it back with an offensive grunt. At last he came to the dog-ticket. His sardonic old French face smiled. 'Et voilà,' he said, clipping the thing and handing it back with a flourish, 'pour Monsieur Toutou!' 'Mr Bow-wow': it seemed to us that the French title was appropriate for our puppy. 'Monsieur Toutou!' we exclaimed; and at the tone of endearment Monsieur Toutou blundered in our direction, pausing only to water the carpet on the way.

It was disappointing to find that other people did not share our satisfaction. Thurber has a passage about naming a dog in which he gives examples of idiotic names: Home Fried; Three Fifteen; Thanks for the Home Run, Emil. But Thurber is concerned chiefly with the impact of the name on the dog; he does not bother about the impact on the dog-owner's circle. We had forgotten that the English look on fancy dog-names with the moral disapproval which they bestow on late rising or good cooking. Monsieur Toutou? Our acquaintances drew back shocked. And indeed even to us Monsieur Toutou began soon to seem a flimsy title for an animal so solid.

On his first evening with us I went downstairs, and

the puppy discovered that the earth was not flat. He had never looked at a staircase before, but the fear of solitude triumphed over vertigo; nose flat between front paws, he peered down for a moment, then plunged heroically over the top step. In a few days he could scramble upstairs as well as down, but always, we noticed, with back legs locked rigidly together. Something about his enthusiastic lollopings reminded us of Disney's fond creature. Pluto, we said, let's call him Pluto. The puppy responded with his usual warmth. But our acquaintances were not appeased. Pluto, said their expression, it's not fair on the poor brute. Perhaps we ourselves were still not sure that we had found a name perfectly apt. At any rate a week or two later we renamed our dog. Coco! we cried suddenly, and wondered, as one often wonders when the simple answer to a problem is found, why we had not thought of it sooner. So Coco it was: cocoa by colour, Coco by nature: Coco the clown.

Authorities say that the poodle is a breed of great antiquity, and while I am not of those who hold that Cerberus was simply an overgrown specimen of the family, I must accept the evidence that Dürer had met poodles and that Jan Steen had seen one dance.

For centuries these dogs have been trained, on the one hand to hunt, on the other to do circus tricks, in either case to be obedient. We started, then, with a puppy inclined by heredity to do what he was told. What astonished us was the quickness with which he grasped what he was being told. That he should answer to his name did not seem extraordinary— though sometimes when I hear the vain cries of other dog-owners in the Park I wonder if I have not taken too much for granted. That he should understand the word Sit did not startle us, though we were gratified when he learned it at the age of ten weeks. But his capacity for not making a nuisance of himself was naturally applauded in a working household such as ours. 'Go to your cushion!' I would say, desperately. Something in the note and number of the words told him that this was no time for joking; dejectedly he would creep to the corner by the stove, thump down and stay there.

Silence and immobility were more easily taught than hygiene. A waiter in a Paris restaurant once assured us, as he laid before us a plate of raspberries soused in some liqueur or other, that he had well watered them: 'je les ai bien arrosées'. Coco certainly watered our house: the rug in the study, the felt in the hall, the carpet on the stairs. At the slightest pause in his gambols we snatched him up in our arms and ran to the terrace at the back of the house (we did not dare to risk the longer journey to the front door); we were never in time. At night he was all self-control. He slept as a puppy on the bed. We would leave him curled on a cushion beside it, but sooner or later there would be a lonely whimpering, he would point out that he could not jump, and without any pretence at self-help he would be lifted up. Once he was on the bed all was safe. And there was no nonsense about early rising. Among my objections to the plan of keeping a dog had been that walk at dawn to the corner of the street. Coco never wanted to get up in the morning; he stayed in bed until we got up, and later. But once he was up the controls were off. For a month we struggled; wheedling, remonstrating, finally resorting to sternness; at each lapse we put him on the terrace and shut the door. He looked bewildered at first, then indignant, then piteous; whined, yapped, scratched the door wildly. When we brought him in he was still sobbing, and it was all we could do to console him.

By the end of the month the meaning of our

puzzling rebukes had dawned on him; after Christmas that year we had no more elementary trouble, and the refinements came fairly easily. It was much longer before the problem of diet was satisfactorily solved.

When we became Coco-owners I inquired carefully from his breeder about his meals. A saucer of wheat-flakes and milk for breakfast, I was told; a saucer of semolina pudding for lunch; two ounces of chopped, cooked rabbit and more semolina pudding for supper. The first day Coco ate his wheat-flakes; the milk pudding, too, went down well. The meat did not so much go down as disappear. The saucer was set on the floor, the muzzle passed over it once, and there was no trace of chopped cooked rabbit. For a few more days the wheat-flakes were accepted, though with dwindling interest. At the end of a week Coco began to look at them with pained surprise. In a fortnight he was through with wheat-flakes. We raised the meat-ration. Again there was the conjurer's pass with the muzzle, accompanied by an instantaneous sound of sucking. It was as if the seventeen-year locust had gone by.

When he was about three months old I took him to the vet; it was, as a matter of fact, to ask about distemper inoculations. At least half-a-pound of rabbit or horseflesh a day, said the vet, try him with pieces of brown bread baked hard in the oven, and make it two meals instead of three. The increase in meat was well received, and for a time Coco agreed to crunch his nuggets of desiccated bread. But before long he was treating them with playful contempt, tossing them in the air and leaving them lying under the study table. His attention was given instead to a vast and, we hoped, indestructible bone at which he sawed all day with puppy teeth.

He grew enormously in height, but he remained, as the vet repeatedly and reproachfully told me, very thin. By the time Coco was six months old I had my orders again: a pound of meat a day, brown bread, a pint of milk, and try a little malt and codliver oil; smear it on his nose so that he will have to lick it off. The brown bread was left in the gravy. A little of the milk was drunk, but only to please me. But the malt and codliver oil excited boundless enthusiasm. No need to smear it on his nose; he almost swallowed the spoon.

But beneath his wool he was still skinny. Officious strangers counted his ribs and traced with their fingers the course of his backbone. If that were *my* dog, they said, I should give him . . . and the suggestions grew: cheese, Virol, carrots, whalemeat, Bovril on toast. The fact was that as far as food was concerned Coco was nobody's dog. His affectionate obedience was, as I have just said, sometimes stronger than his feeling (shared by more children than the dieticians suspect) that milk in large quantities is a dull drink. He would take a lap from the pannikin I held for him, sheer away, circle round the table, then come shambling back; at the third round he would down the lot. But little by little he chose his own menu and arranged his own meals. Meat, he made clear (and in this he merely seconded the instructions of the vet) was the stuff for him. He liked one large meal a day, not two; he preferred it in the evening, not in the morning; in short he liked eating late in company with us. At midday he took a snack: a mouthful of cheese, perhaps, preferably Gorgonzola, or a little smoked haddock, or half-a-dozen potted shrimps if they were going; if nothing on our frugal table pleased him he would be content with his regular lunch, a handful of dog biscuits, and no nonsense about wholemeal rusks. He dined by our side at half-past seven: a pound of meat, horse, rabbit or tinned meat, garnished with vegetables; afterwards

20

he lay extended in the study until midnight, dreaming and digesting, a process which when he was young was accompanied by a loud and indeed alarming sound of panting. When he came to he was ready for a frisk before, at one o'clock or two, he followed us to bed.

This happy equilibrium, however, was not reached until he was almost grown up. Long before then we had met the first real crisis in life with Coco.

3

A PAIR OF JOURNALISTS such as Leonard and myself look on the evening after dinner as part of the working day. But now and then, perhaps once a week, we dine out, and we soon had to make up our minds what, on these occasions, we should do with the puppy. Where Coco was concerned I was the disciplinarian of the family. If I had to have a dog I wanted a dog who would give me no trouble. All the same it was by common consent that the first time we went out in the evening we left him in the kitchen. He was not quite solitary. A kitten of his own age shared the basement with him; but our maids slept at the top of the house and would be out of earshot. It had not entered our heads that a puppy snatched no more than a week or two earlier from his family could not be expected to accept his isolation with fortitude. We must try, I said, to get the dog used to being left alone.

We hurried home early after dinner. Up to that moment, though I had felt an owner's anxiety if the puppy refused his breakfast or by accident swallowed a spike of rabbit bone, I had not thought I was personally entangled. We opened the front door. There was not a sound in the house; and suddenly a pang of affection for the dependent little creature struck me. Was it possible that in desperation he had struggled up the stairs from the kitchen, had fallen, and now lay with a broken paw on the passage linoleum? The disciplinarian flew to the door, opened it and turned on the light. It was like coming out of a tunnel to see Coco standing at the foot of the stairs, silent as if detected in some misdemeanour, but smiling ingratiatingly.

The experiment gave us more confidence than was proper. At any rate on four more evenings we left Coco in the kitchen. Once we were late; it was the first night of 'Venus Observed', and we had supped after the theatre with the Harold Hobsons, but when we looked down the stairs to the basement the fawn body was still there, indefatigably wagging. It was to be the last occasion for felicitations. A week later we came home from dining with friends to find a note on the mat. A neighbour could not sleep for the noise of Coco's woe. The dog, said her note, barked incessantly. Other people too, it added, were kept awake; no doubt I was unaware of the nuisance he was. Next morning I learned that the house had been in an uproar, the telephone ringing with appeals from my correspondent for quiet, and Nancy and Ennis brought down from their eyrie to answer her rings at the door-bell. I went to apologize. My tone froze when the distracted complainant insisted that Coco cried every night of the week. But in future he obviously could not be left alone. His entry into society was thus untimely hastened.

In the three months since Coco forsook his family to ride home with me he had almost doubled in size. The body beneath the silky fluff stood on long straight legs; and when he went to the Park with Leonard's sister Doddie there was now something about the head vaguely reminiscent of his species. All the same he was a long way from the appearance of a poodle. Once when I took him to the vet for inoculation against distemper I asked whether we should have his coat trimmed. Leave it for a bit, said the vet; he'll lose his puppy fur anyway. We came to take it for granted that our dog should look like an eager hearthrug. And we began to regard what we thought were his shortcomings with indulgence. Long after he came to live with us he was still plopping up and down stairs with hind legs locked together. For months he could not manage the easy hop on to the bed. At first he was lifted bodily, then he climbed, one leg at a time. We made extravagant demonstrations of the running jump. He ran accommodatingly with us to the bed, then pulled up with a bewildered air. Perhaps, we said, he will never learn to jump. We even wondered, as we watched him sitting with one haunch askew, whether there was something wrong with his back legs. We were always ready to assume that something was wrong, never that anything might be right.

Anything, that is, except his character—and his obedience. I was at that time much teased about being sentimental over Coco's youth. When anybody admired him, 'He's only a puppy', I said, voice trembling with pride in his accomplishments. The words became a domestic catch-phrase; 'He's only a puppy', Leonard would murmur ironically at some display of only moderate sagacity. But Leonard was as ready as I was to beam on Coco's good manners as a guest. A few days after our disgrace with the neighbours we were to dine with Elizabeth Nicholas and her husband. Elizabeth belongs to the large class of human beings who do not dote on dogs; as a matter of fact I think she is one of the smaller group who are indifferent to all animals. Though I do not share it, I understand her point of view, especially where other people's animals are concerned. One can usually rely on their killing conversation as well as injuring the furniture. To ask if we might bring a five-months-old puppy to dinner was an imposition. To leave him at home alone (since Nancy and Ennis were out) meant insomnia in Albion Street. As always when faced with a what-should-A-do situation I prevailed on Leonard to handle the affair; his frank attack and natural good humour succeed where my elaborate circumlocutions produce nothing but an awkward pause. 'Dear,' I could hear him telephoning, 'we have a great treat for you . . .' Half an hour later Coco, dressed in a nurseling's red harness, was being hauled into a taxi.

Elizabeth's little Regency house was newly decorated and newly furnished, and at the sight of her speckless carpets I felt, I confess, abashed. But Coco's manners were equal to the occasion. He lay where he was told, shambled downstairs at my heels and curled noiselessly in a corner during dinner, obligingly remained with the gentlemen when the ladies withdrew, and for the rest of the evening allowed us to forget his existence. 'He's only a puppy', said Leonard as we drove home. But next morning he it was who gave Doddie an embellished account of the dog's poise.

From that moment Coco was a regular diner-out. He came with us to the houses of our friends; he came with us to restaurants—or perhaps I should say to a restaurant, for we began to limit ourselves to one or two where we knew he would be welcome. At the White Tower our friend Yanni Stais or his brother Alec could be counted on to give us a discreet table for two and a dog. We urged Coco out of the taxi, gave sixpence to the violinist under the street-lamp and entered, somewhat impeded by our companion's anxiety to extend his greetings in person to every diner in the place. But once we were in our corner there was no more trouble. A look, no more, was occasionally exchanged with the Michael Denisons' dog, then Coco settled down under the table for the evening. He was much clucked at by other diners and much petted by the staff, who brought him bowls of water and titbits. But he did not stray from

C

our feet, and when we left, often with a large parcel of bones presented by the patron, we bore ourselves with modest pride.

There were, of course, evenings when it was not possible for him to share our engagements, and then Nancy and Ennis volunteered to keep him company. He dined with them in the basement and climbed early to bed on the top floor; he was asleep long before we came home. But he soon learned to recognize the ping of a taximeter in the street. We banged the front door to let him know that the taxi was ours and nobody else's, wiped our feet on the mat, and waited. Far off, high up, there was a sound of pattering. It slowed down and stopped while Coco, somewhere upstairs, stood wondering in the dark silent house if he had made a mistake. We called softly. The pattering began again, grew louder, like an avalanche gathering speed. Coco almost threw himself down the last flight of stairs before he rushed at us, bouncing off us and back again in a paroxysm of welcome.

I must not let it be supposed that he was always a guest and never a host. He was from the beginning delighted to see visitors in the house. Unlike his mistress, he never shrank from human company, never wondered what had possessed him to give a party. The demands on his social technique, perhaps, were small. He dined before the guests arrived; during the gin and the introductions he was absent-minded, and when we went into the dining-room he was ready to stretch out, indifferent to the problems of conversation or carving. By the time he woke up, food and drink had relaxed us all, and the company was indulgent.

I do not remember what suggested to us that his gifts might be employed outside the domestic circle. But Leonard, always an encourager of young talent, it was who made the first move towards preparing Coco for a career by calling in Howard Byrne to take a photograph. The moment was not particularly auspicious. Coco's youth, like the youth of many distinguished people, had been and still was chequered by unusual illnesses. I pass over the inelegant canine indispositions; Coco, soaring above these, contracted tonsillitis. He had also an affection of the ears which demanded oil treatment and the removal of super-fluous hair. 'People don't like doing it,' said the vet, 'because they're afraid of hurting the dog; but it's much better for you to pull a little out every day rather than my pulling a lot out once a month, and' (appealing to my vanity) 'I can see you'll be sensible'. Coco grunted while I pulled tufts of fluff from the convolutions of his ears; and Leonard spooned in liquid paraffin which presently oozed out again, staining neck and cheeks grey. Can we bath him? I asked. The vet was discouraging; we compromised on a trim. Before he sat for his portrait, then, Coco went off for his first barbering and, after an altercation between me and a frustrated beauty specialist, came home neat but still grubby. The trim was roughly but not precisely that known as the Astrakhan; our dog now had short woolly curls all over his head, body and legs, a knob on the end of his tail, and long silk-fringed ears. The photograph, in colour, was taken against a background of bookshelves: Leonard, literary in canary-coloured shirt with hunting-stock, examined a book while Coco in his red harness stood on a window seat and pretended to read too. He might have been less studious had not a potato crisp been hidden between the pages of the book. But as things were he posed as obligingly and as professionally as any film star. And yet he was, as Leonard once more reminded me, still only a puppy.

4

PERHAPS THE VERY FACT that we were willing to put our pet on paper, as it were, shows that we were growing less despondent about his looks. A week or two after this early appearance before the camera I even went so far as to use the word poodle in public. I was giving a broadcast. The subject was Cats and Dogs, and in sketching my acquaintance with Coco I described the effect of his first visit to the barber. 'We went in,' I said, 'with what looked like a sheep-dog, and came out with something distinctly resembling a poodle'. And yet when I look at the photograph which appeared in Leonard's 'Saturday Book' that year, all I see is a rather dirty rough-haired terrier with the wrong ears.

The broadcast showed that I was changing my mind about something other than Coco's figure. The point of the talk was that, once exclusively devoted to cats, I had come round to dogs—or rather to a dog—as well. There had been a change, too, in our domestic circle since the days when I was resisting the importation of a puppy. My old friend Perry had gone from us. I try to persuade myself that his end was unclouded by jealousy, that I was not to blame for bringing home in the last days not only Coco, but a black kitten as well. I do not convince myself. It is true that Perry's attitude towards the newcomers betrayed nothing but disgust. And yet I am afraid he was hurt. We tried to tell him that nobody could take his place; he looked at us sourly and snuffled. He had been ill for months: too old, said the vet, too old for drastic cures; now the elegant body moved stiffly, and he could scarcely breathe for catarrh. One morning Nancy and Ennis, who cared fondly for him, called me to the kitchen. He was in a bad way, they said; but he roused himself to answer my caresses, purred and turned in my arms and rubbed his whiskers against my cheek. A week later he went with me once more to the vet. It was, though I hoped against hope, his last visit, and I went back alone to a household in tears.

Coco in the first months of his life thus was free from the acrimony of elderly rivals. With the human race he had from the start no difficulties. He bore the separation from his brothers and sisters with enthusiasm, and tucked himself into Leonard's life and mine as if it were his own. Routine and interruptions to routine were equally welcome. He sat with us at lunch in the study or came downstairs to dinner; but when soon after his arrival influenza struck the house he sprawled happily all day long on Leonard's bed. The invalid said he had never known a more consoling visitor.

Our guests were as much impressed by his social confidence as by his obedience. When he waggled trustingly up to one of our friends, a psychiatrist used to misfits, 'He must,' said the observer in a surprised tone, as if he expected a juvenile delinquent, 'he must feel very secure'. Somebody else—I think it was Hugh Massingham—asked how we trained him to be so well behaved. 'Oh,' I said, purring at the flattery, 'hot irons, you know'. But to tell the truth there had been, once the principles of hygiene had been instilled, little training to be done. I have already remarked that the dog soon grasped what we wanted him to do. It seemed to us that he had, as well as a quick intelligence, an inherited memory. He did not have to be taught to follow at heel. We took him out, and he followed at heel.

One day in the house, feeling the need not to be followed, I thought of my instructions when his mother accompanied me into the buzz of Notting Hill Gate—a finger across the nose means: Wait till I tell you. I laid my hand on Coco's muzzle and said 'Stay!' When I came back into the room two minutes later he was still there, thumping with his tail and asking if he could get up now. That evening we almost offered our dog as a study for the biologists, Lysenko not excluded.

But Coco had also to come to terms with his own kind, and first of all with his contemporary the kitten. I had brought the two young creatures to the house on the selfsame day; they would, I hoped, grow up together as friends. The kitten, a self-contained little animal from a farm where with his brothers he had run wild and foraged for himself, had no fear of dogs. As for Coco, all he wanted was a playfellow. At the first encounter he trotted up to the stranger, who neatly and without haste withdrew to the arm of a chair and sat staring coldly with golden eyes. But it was not long before the kitten was making the advances. The name given him by Nancy and Ennis was Smut: a traditional name with an ironic echo, for the great eunuch cat whom Perry had so rudely set about was called Smut too; his owner with unconscious truth had sometimes addressed him as 'Mutt. There was nothing of the mutt about our kitten. He was, when he first met Coco, about half the puppy's size. In two months half had become a quarter, and the quarter was boss. The two animals did not live closely together. The kitten found our life in the study too smoky and febrile for his taste, but when they met he it was who took command. He swaggered up, arched his back and wove to and fro, reared on hind legs to rub his head under Coco's chin, flung himself down and swung insolently on the long fur of Coco's legs. Sometimes, making himself as tall as he could, he walked backwards and forwards under the puppy's belly. Coco stood taut, not daring to move, his tail wagging and his whole body trembling with a delicious mixture of terror and tickling. Occasionally in a burst of animal spirits (a phrase which for the first time in our lives we fully understood) he chased the kitten down the passage to the scullery; when he got his nose smacked he merely blinked and shrank away with a look of faint surprise. Once he fell into disgrace for a game on the landing upstairs, when Smut, performing some virtuoso's balancing feat, slipped through the banisters and landed, shaken but mercifully unhurt, a floor below. But as Coco grew older he learned respect for a cat's fast punches, and within a twelvemonth he would scarcely dare to pass the kitten on the stairs.

Meanwhile the outside world of animals had to be faced. Not that Coco was in the least reluctant; until disillusioned he felt as secure with a dog as with a man. The earliest encounters took place in Hyde Park. Before his entry into the family we had hardly noticed the presence of the Park at the end of the street, but we soon learned how handy it is to have a dog's local. Coco set off on a lead. From infancy he flung up his feet in the Hackney action expected of a poodle, combining the movement, however, with a tendency to turn his toes in; as he went down the street he rolled slightly, with an amiable nautical air. Once the Park was reached his escort let him off the lead and he raced away. Before long he had made a number of friends. Girls were his favourites, among them a miniature poodle whom he treated with the utmost gallantry, lying on his back with feet in the air and allowing her to jump on his stomach. The owners of these playmates, at first alarmed by his relative size (even at four months a standard poodle towers over a full-grown miniature), soon felt relief when he appeared on the morning walk; their pets would come to no harm with him. As a matter of fact any miniature poodle could outdistance Coco, and when at the end of the mad circling race the contestants set to boxing, any miniature could bowl him over. His great paws never hurt anyone, and the owners who stood round watching the tourney cried to my delighted ears: 'What a gentleman!'

Not all his town acquaintances were as urbanely playful. I remember a dinner in a friend's house when the resident poodle persisted all evening in mistaking Coco's gentlemanly manners for the coyness of a girl. His rural acquaintances again were a different matter.

Since the autumn of 1948 Leonard and I had been in the habit of spending our week-ends in the country. On Saturday we bolted out of the house, each with a grip full of books, and caught a train for Kent. On Sunday we came back further burdened at my insistence with an ill-tied bundle of wild flowers, usually of some type catalogued by the botanists in the phrase: *hedges and waste ground; common; fl. all summer*. The pursuit of this simple booty gave me inexplicable pleasure, and Leonard never complained.

During our week-ends we lodged at a farm. The village was tiny, life was gentle, and we dropped into a rhythm in which a five-mile bus-ride seemed an adventure; most days we found distraction enough in walking across the pasture where the white mare grazed, down the winding road over the brook, back again past the big field with the lapwings crying, past the church, the inn and the cottage garden full of cats. If we had not fallen into the habit of that walk we might not have felt the need to acquire Coco.

The farm when we first knew it had two Alsatian bitches, mother and daughter. The daughter, a young charmer called Dusky, attached herself to us, and we asked if we might take her with us on our round. She was quite undisciplined. At the stir of a rabbit's foot she was off, and we shouted ourselves hoarse while she crashed about in the woods or dug vast earthworks. A quarter of an hour later she came back without the rabbit, grinning apologetically, her nose and tongue ochre with earth from the warrens by the stream. We persuaded her to follow at heel after a fashion. She enjoyed the outings, and we took pleasure in her wayward company. I said at the beginning of this story that an early prejudice had been partly broken down before I met Coco. Dusky it was who convinced me that it might be worth while to have a dog, and I felt melancholy, the week-end before we went off on our summer holidays, at the thought of leaving her behind. She felt melancholy herself. At any rate she tried to come to the station, and as we trudged off with our bags of books and our cow-parsnip we looked back to see her straining away from the cowman's hand at her collar and turning her head to watch us. The next time we went to the farm she was gone. Dusky was not a child-lover, and there had been trouble, I am sure not of her making, with trespassing children from a neighbouring farm: the kind of trouble for which a long, an endless sleep is the only sure remedy. For a week or two our walk across the field and back by the church seemed tasteless.

When Coco joined the family circle it was part of our plan that he should replace Dusky as a week-end companion, and in no time at all we were taking him with us on our Saturday journey. To our relief he behaved with composure in train and taxi and showed no disquiet in a strange house. Somebody had advised me always to take with me a puppy rug or a blanket to make him feel at home, something at any rate which he would recognize as his own; on the first Saturday a cushion was added to our luggage. Coco ignored the thing, and we quickly gave up pretending that he was attached to anything but our presence. Once more he settled down without any fuss: slept on the bed, got up when we got up, stretched before the fire in the sitting-room. On our first visit we did not venture to take him on our familiar walk. That, we argued, might be too far for a puppy not yet three months old who until a week or two earlier had lived in a shed and exercised in a back yard. The next week-end we took the risk. Again he reassured us, trotting jauntily at our side without tiring.

The winter dragged by. With spring the farm was full of young animals and birds: white kids, ducklings and goslings, a little pig snorting in the greenhouse. Coco learned that the farm creatures were not for play. Once warned, he ceased to gambol after the ducks, ignored the hens which pecked through the garden fence, and kept his distance from the savage geese and the tethered goats. At first we were anxious about his behaviour with the larger animals. If he met a herd of cows he was likely to bound towards it. His mad zigzagging in the field offended the old white mare too; once or twice she lumbered in his direction, and we remembered the malignant speed with which the slowest horse can swivel to strike with its heels. We were a little uneasy even about Dawn, the remaining Alsatian. We need not have worried. The handsome bitch took the puppy's advances in good part, repulsing him with a warning only when his impertinences went beyond bounds, and as he grew she began in a womanly way to defer to him. Within a year he was greeting her with brisk condescension. Before this he had learned to take no notice of cattle or horses—or indeed of the sheep which cropped the sooty summer grass in Hyde Park.

But none of these were openly hostile. Some people preen themselves on preferring in social matters the frontal to the concealed attack: 'I don't mind what they say to my face as long as they don't say it behind my back'. Coco, like many civilized and sensitive beings, abhorred the direct affront. One spring afternoon I took him for a walk in a strange direction; as we came to an oast-house on a hill, from the stockyard two dogs rushed out, choking with fury. Coco did not hesitate for a second; he lowered his tail, tucked in his rump, and bolted up the hill. In vain

I called, in vain demonstrated that the two attackers would run for cover at the wave of an arm; he was still bolting. I was full of upbraiding as I took him back to the farm. And yet Coco behaved with excellent sense. He wanted no arguments, and he had offered none. We asked, as I presently reflected, a great deal of our puppy. We wanted him to be no trouble; we wanted him to be a companion; and at the same time we expected him to behave like a dog's dog. The only thing, as I see now, which we were ready to waive was chic. We did not insist on the appearance of a poodle.

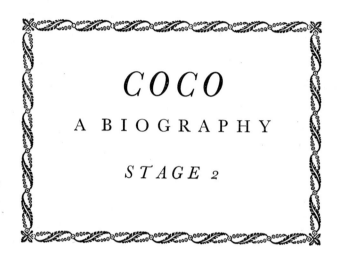

COCO

A BIOGRAPHY

STAGE 2

D

5

IN SOME WAYS Coco's education was well advanced by the time the first winter was past. At six months he had mastered the routine of urban domesticity; he had learned to mix with his own kind and with the human race. In the four months since he became a member of our household my reluctance to own a dog had been completely overcome. He had won our private hearts; but it was a surprise to find him making conquests of his own. And by this I mean friends outside his circle of acquaintances in the Park and up and down the street.

We were invited that year to spend Easter in Hampshire with our friends the Woodham-Smiths; Cecil Woodham-Smith was then awaiting the publication of her biography of Florence Nightingale. The family owned an exquisite Siamese cat who abominated dogs. If the Emperor, they said, hears a dog barking five miles away he sits up and spits. But they were ready to sacrifice the Emperor's comfort to hospitality. Coco was asked too, and amidst Imperial oaths we led him across the threshold of their country house.

Welcome, said Cecil, to the wireless poodle. We looked inquiring. Since the broadcast, she said, everybody here has been wanting to see the wireless poodle. Allowances must be made for the exaggerations of affection, and everybody was, I think, selected from Cecil's friendly staff of daily helpers. But what interested me was not that an audience in a rural district of Hampshire should have listened to the broadcast on Cats and Dogs to which I referred just now. I am not vain of my performance on the air. Like many broadcasters, I usually come away feeling that I have made an irredeemable ass of myself. I am however given to the belief that my broadcasts are my own and the producer's. But here the broadcaster was ignored. Nobody cared about the wireless speaker; what mattered was the wireless poodle. And not in Hampshire only. Acquaintances met by chance in the train, I found, would scarcely bother to greet me. 'Oh,' they would say, brushing me aside, 'is this Coco?' I began to fancy that he had given the broadcast himself.

Among the general public he was making friends; but at the Woodhams' he found a private tough nut. The first hours of our visit the Emperor spent snaking from cover to cover; from the shelter of a table or a chair his black three-cornered mask looked furiously out. The Lucifer look never changed, and yet I could have sworn the face was convulsed with contempt and loathing. Coco was puzzled. The smack on the nose he understood; passive malevolence was new to him. But after one or two movements of affable inquiry, which we checked, he settled down, laid his muzzle on his paws and asked no more questions. Frantic, the Emperor sprang on to precarious ledges, flipped the tulips in their bowl with an insolent hand, or hung scrabbling with all his claws to peep over the back of the settee. Coco never stirred.

Within twenty-four hours the Emperor's abhorrence was dwindling to curiosity. He began to follow Coco from room to room; he could not believe that any animal could be at once so rumbustious and so harmless. He put his head round doors; he glided up when Coco was stretched out and sniffed delicately at the monster's feet. One night Leonard and I were reading in bed. The household was asleep, no light shone but ours, and there was not a sound except the faint purring and spitting of our dying wood fire. Suddenly in the midnight stillness our bedroom door flew open. Who's there? I whispered; but it was no ghost, only the Emperor, come to see how Coco spent the night.

He must, I fear, have observed that the visitor slept sprawling on the eiderdown. Later, when size and weight made Coco an impossible bedfellow, we prevailed on him to sleep on a rug on the floor. But at this time he used to lie across our feet; easiest of hosts, the Woodhams knew and did not mind. He had by now got the knack of jumping on to a bed. What is more, he no longer went downstairs in a series of bounces with his rear locked. His hind legs had learned to operate independently of one another; at least, we said, remembering our early forebodings, there's nothing wrong with them. All the same he still sat very oddly, as if he had difficulty in managing so many legs, and such long ones, at a time. And in other ways he did not seem to be growing up. At six months he was a heavy young animal, bony but powerful beneath his wool. But that did not stop him from scrambling on to Leonard's lap for protection. As he sat there he blotted out his nurse.

'Coco thinks,' said Cecil, 'he's still a dear little thing'. The Emperor crept nearer to have a look, and stopped short only of jumping on the same knees. A day later, though he did not share a lap, he was sharing a couch. Leonard was in bed with influenza. When visitors came to condole, they found they were not the first; there, extended on the eiderdown in an ecstasy of comfort, one on each side of the invalid, were Coco and the Emperor.

The encounter with the Woodhams' Siamese cat might, I suppose, be regarded as Coco's first acquaintance with foreigners, and the visit to Hampshire was the beginning of his Grand Tour. He reacted to it in the fashion of many a young man making a first visit to the Continent: he over-ate. There was a picnic in Savernake Forest, a *déjeuner sur l'herbe* more solidly dressed, perhaps, than Manet's but no less light-hearted; Easter ramblers in the woods stared to see a Siamese cat prowling through the bracken and a lamb-coloured puppy enjoying a meal of ham sandwiches, sausage rolls, hard-boiled eggs and shortbread. It would have seemed heartless to keep the pair of them out of anything that afternoon, and later, when we came to Inkpen Beacon, we all climbed together up the hillside. Coco ran with ears streaming behind him in the wind, while the Emperor moved stealthily, as if he missed the cover of the jungle, and paused every now and then to shake the touch of the turf from a delicate paw. 'This', said Cecil, 'is a historic occasion. It must be the first time a Siamese cat has walked over Inkpen Beacon'.

It was days before Coco recovered from his over-indulgence. He, of course, learned no lesson. But we tried after that to resist his appeals for a human diet. It was not easy. The family was sometimes divided on the question, and I became the martinet to escape whose vigilance was an affectionate joke. It grew no easier as time went on, for in the society in which Coco increasingly moved there was a tendency to offer him anything he fancied, from a boiled sweet to a lick of rum; if he found the taste displeasing he sat back and gave a loud click of his teeth. One thing, however, we felt we could do to equip him for the social round: send him to the tailor and cutter. He had recovered from the ear-and-throat trouble which had been a handicap at his first visit to the barber. He was well enough and old enough to be bathed. But first we had to agree on a hair-cut. There were long conferences. Should we stick to the Astrakhan Trim or should we venture

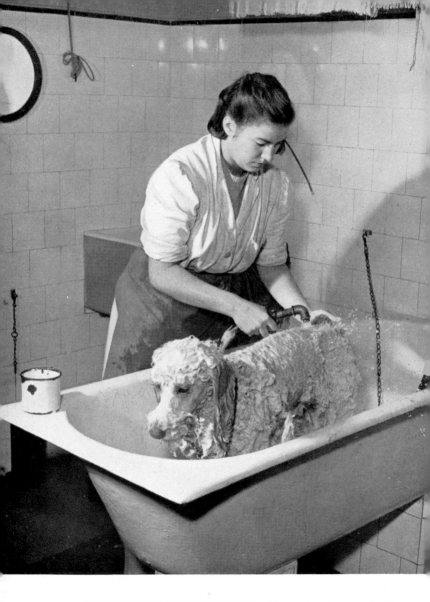

THE 'EAGER HEARTHRUG' on the previous page eventually
underwent the ordeal by water. He emerged (opposite) looking
like a poodle at last

on the Puppy Clip, the Lamb Trim or the Royal Dutch (or Modern) Trim? We were sure of one thing, that whatever the dog-fanciers might say we would never subject Coco to the traditional Lion Clip, in which the dog wears a heavy fur bolero with a naked midriff, and exposes close-trimmed buttocks (the Continental Clip insists on a naked rear). He was in any case far too young for an adult wardrobe, though by the time we had decided to take the advice of the barber he was almost eight months old.

I don't know what I expected to see when at the end of the day I called at the Dog Bath Shop where I had left Coco in the morning. I said just now that we had a lamb-coloured puppy. Since he had been in the family he had paled. When he adopted us we had called him apricot, but in six months he had lost much of his fawn, and by early summer his wool, unwashed and sooty from the Park, had the greyish look of a dirty sheep. It had not struck me that this was anything but his natural colour. As for his silhouette, I had not supposed that trimming would change it. I had not given any hard-and-fast instructions: a sort of Dutch Trim, I said, not too much off his middle, and left it feebly at that. Certainly I expected to know my own dog. After all, he had been to the barber before and had returned recognizable.

It had been a busy day, and I went straight to Beauchamp Place from a committee meeting. I gave my name; I've come, I said, for Coco. Oh yes, I was told, he's ready for you. There was a pause while an attendant went behind the scenes and I looked at studded collars, models of dog-bathrooms, and signed photographs of grateful champions. Presently there was a rattling of toenails, and the attendant came back leading a dazzling golden-white dog with a close-cropped midriff, vast fluffy shoulders and haunches, shaven cheeks and heavy beard and moustaches. But that, I said, isn't my . . . I was not allowed to finish the denial; for the splendid creature, panting with affectionate delight, flung himself into my arms.

I walked along Knightsbridge in a dog-owner's ferment. Excited by his release, Coco bounced at my side; people on the pavement nudged one another and turned round to admire. Our progress across the Park was all triumph. Everybody stopped to smile at Coco, prancing heraldically under the trees in his new red collar. In the late afternoon sun he was the dancing fleece.

I looked at him: the pudding-basin hair-cut above the long neck, the deep chest sloping away into the narrow belly, the pom-pom on the tail, the immense cowboy chaps, and the shaven, exposed look round the eyes which, as Leonard presently said, gave a touch of melancholy to his face—with Coco's first long pants our domestic situation had changed. Up to that moment we had been inclined to apologize for our puppy. To us he might have become everything that was amiable, intelligent and charming, but we could not pretend that he was smart. Now it was for my own appearance that I felt I ought to apologize. I was not dressed, and I very much doubted whether I should find that Leonard was dressed, for taking this mirror of fashion out for a walk. I felt, too, that we ought to apologize to Coco for questioning his breeding. For six months we had doubted, and now at the end we were in possession of just such a creature, whiskers and all, as we had admired years earlier. After all we had a poodle.

6

NOT EVERYBODY SHARED our delight in Coco's haircut. Six months earlier we might ourselves have thought it too modish, and six months before that we should have vowed that no puppy of ours should be trimmed at all. But life with a poodle easily accustoms you to the bizarre, and now we defended our taste with arrogance against acquaintances who thought we had, in their own phrase, made the dog look a fool. Doddie, taking him for his morning prance in the Park, for a day or two had a hard time of it with other dog-walkers who missed the old shaggy silhouette. But the strangeness wore off—and the clipped coat grew. In any case children, always among Coco's admirers, accepted his new shape without complaint or even comment. One child remarked that the dog had had pieces cut out of him; the rest simply flung their arms round his neck. Occasionally little boys, collecting dog-types

54

as others collect car-numbers, would ask what breed he was. And once a schoolboy gave Doddie some advice on exhibiting a dog. 'You ought to show him,' he told her, 'but you must begin with a small show and work up to the big shows'.

I daresay Coco would have been the perfect pet for a house full of children. Sweet-tempered and incomparably woolly, he never failed to waggle up to any child who called him, or to suffer as long as solicited its ill-aimed pats and strokes. He did not draw back even when some baby young enough to be top-heavy staggered towards him, lost her balance and, seeing his head level with her own, steadied herself by his ears. But in his heart he would have preferred a world without children. He played his part, of course, in the social round. When we dined with Ruth McKenney it was his job to entertain Ruth's little girl, who was too young to stay up for dinner. Off he shambled to the bedroom, but with drooping head and backward glance; and I shall not forget the look of appeal he gave us when the Denis Hamiltons brought their four boys, ranging in age from ten to four, to spend Whit Monday at the farm. That, I remember, was the day when a child fell in the ornamental pond in the garden of the

'Henry VIII', Hever's charming pub. A complacent little girl in a party frock and bronze ringlets, she had been squeaking with a playmate on the farther verge; there was a terrified howl, and she was stuck in the reeds like a fly in beer-froth. I set off round the pond at a trot. But arriving first at the scene of the accident is a matter not of speed but of character. I have long accepted the fact that I am no rescuer, and I was not surprised to see Denis Hamilton sprint past me, splash into the reeds and come out with the child unhurt in his arms.

I wish I could record that Coco had joined the rescue party. But to tell the truth he was in need of rescue himself. He had been delivered into the hands of the Hamilton boys; all day long they had alternately chased and embraced him. As we drove up the road for tea I could see him sitting in the back of the car, peeping gloomily from a nest of little boys; when we got out he ran, vainly of course, to hide behind my skirts. His relief was unconcealed when our young guests, still huzzaing for Coco, set off on their journey back to London.

In any case he was not a rescuer either. His nature shrank from the risks incurred in saving anybody from anything. Indeed it shrank from risks of any kind. Watching him bounce back from some unfamiliar object—a coat-hanger, for instance—I could not help contrasting him with my old Siamese companion. Perry, faced with the visible unknown, always walked towards it with his nose out. The invisible he greeted with more enthusiasm still. At a cottage where we used to spend week-ends there was a hatch, breast-high and about cat-size, in the door between the kitchen and the dining-room. Perry, shut in the kitchen, did not hesitate. He launched himself at the hole in the door; from the dining-room we saw him arrow through it and land on the narrow ledge on our side. If he saw an unguarded chimney he rushed up it and sat in the dark on the sooty shelf.

Our poodle had none of Perry's adventurousness, and none of his independence; he was the least stoic character I have ever known. That summer we took to walking in the Park after dinner. Dusk, boys stubbornly playing cricket under the trees, and the solemn respiration of London in the distance—against the crepuscular background Coco's demonstration of perpetual motion seemed especially charming. To and fro he scurried, nose to the ground, his fleece glimmering in the colourless light;

occasionally he advanced winningly towards some pair intertwined on the grass, then, called off, tossed his head and cantered away, looking back defiantly over his shoulder. But he was not looking backwards on the evening when he ran full-tilt into an iron chair. The thing was lying on its side, half-folded and thrown down. One minute Coco was tearing ahead with the see-saw, rocking-horse movement which was his expression of joy. The next, flopped on his belly, he was uttering a series of high-pitched, regular, agonized screams. We ran to him. I had seen him crash, and judging from his cries I thought he must have broken four paws at least. We felt his legs; he screamed. We lifted him; he lay down again and screamed. I began to console him as one would console a child. 'Poor Coco!' I said. 'There, there, poor Coco!' He still went on crying, but less shrilly and with a less regular beat. 'There, there,' we urged, 'there, there!' The cries wavered into piteous, long-drawn-out whimpers. Presently he sat up, then amidst our applause got to his feet. He was still whining in a desultory way, but as he moved we were encouraged to think that no great damage had been done. We even began to suspect that he was delaying his recovery in order to prolong our solicitude.

After a few more minutes he ran off. All his legs were working as usual, and he made no further reference to his sufferings. 'Either of us,' said Leonard, 'would have been in hospital for a month'.

The incident gave us another aspect of Coco to reflect on beside his quick healing and his rejection of the principles of stoicism: his eyesight. Couldn't he see the chair ahead of him in the twilight? Occasionally there were hints that his vision fell short of the falcon's. But the time of looking for flaws in our poodle was past. The interest of strangers, the admiration of acquaintances, most of all his own lately revealed elegance were giving us quite other ideas.

Late in June we went on holiday: a week-end in Paris, a fortnight of inertia in the South, then back to Paris to find crowds dancing in the squares and the Boulevard de Clichy got up for the Fourteenth of July in shooting booths, oyster stalls and screeching roundabouts. When we reached London again we looked with new interest at our dog.

The South of France in summer is full not simply of poodles, but of poodle-clipped dogs; everybody who owns a mongrel not by nature bald takes pity on the creature in the heat and shaves its midriff.

E

And that summer there were poodles everywhere: on the trains, in the cafés, on the beaches, where they joyfully flung themselves into the sea and rushed out again, indifferently spattering with water and sand the naked, oily, sun-dazed bodies on the hired mattresses. 'Youki!' screamed the owners. 'Non alors, Youki!' We asked a French family at the hotel about Youki: was it a common name for a dog? Ah, Youki, they said, that was one of the Y names; in order to preserve the purity of the breed poodles born in a certain year would be given names beginning with a certain letter of the alphabet. The point was, I admit, not made clear. But then neither, to our ignorant eyes, was the purity of the breed. Poodles with fringy teeth peeping past the lower lip; poodles with long aimless tails; poodles with square heads and short muzzles—we could not believe that these inharmonious shapes were pure poodle. Coco, we said jealously when we got back to London and he came curvetting out of the house to greet us, Coco has a far better figure than any of them.

It was, to be honest, a figure inclined to sit down for a good scratch. Coco had taken advantage of his holidays to ask in a colony of dog-lice. But after a visit to Beauchamp Place he came home deloused and radiant: radiant enough to make us self-conscious about taking so urban an animal to our rural retreat at the week-end. We had some justification. At the Kentish station Coco as usual bounded out of the train, followed us down the dank subterranean steps under the line and led the way up the other side to the ticket-collector; vast furry hams twinkled as he ran. A countryman nudged his neighbour and turned to stare: 'Look,' he said, 'look at them 'ind-quarters!' But his tone was admiring, and to our pleasure we found that most people who lived in the country, far from despising our dandified pet, took to him at sight. We even began to feel that they accepted us, townspeople though we were, on his account.

We were at the farm for the August Bank Holiday, date of the Agricultural Show at Edenbridge. We had gone to the Show the year before, and we looked back with delight on the spectacle: the marquees, the cars drawn up in the field, the jumping, the procession of amiable bulls and mild cows with their calves, the splendid beribboned dray-horses, the pack of beagles jostling round the ring. This time the kindness of the Isidore Kermans enabled us to sit in the members' enclosure instead of pressing against the ropes.

Luckily Coco was still fresh from the tailor and cutter. His rig-out made up for any failings in ours. Everybody looked at him, nobody bothered about us.

The day's entertainment may have been dull from the point of view of a ten-months-old poodle. Salmon mayonnaise in the hot marquee, then the long afternoon in the sun—there was nothing for him in the traditional rites: the hunter trials, Sam Marsh driving a four-in-hand, and the heroes of the chase blowing their hallowed melancholy notes on the hunting-horn. But Coco was never one to wait supinely to be amused. I said just now that he collected his own circle of human acquaintances in our street and in the Park. He did more: wherever he went he made friends, rushing up to strangers in public places with a confidence embarrassing to our reticence. The afternoon of the Agricultural Show was not wasted. In the intervals of the jumping we would look round: Where's Coco? one of us would ask; and the other would reassure: it's all right, he's just making a few friends. Sometimes his new admirers favoured us with a nod or a smile; sometimes they included us in the conversation. At last somebody asked a question. Among the early events of the day there had been a dog show, with anything in the ring from a Great Dane to a tiny mincer. Our neighbour on the row of chairs looked at Coco's creamy fleece: 'Have you been showing him?' he asked.

Had we been showing him? The schoolboy's advice on dog shows came back to us. We thought of the Mediterranean breeds, we remembered the starers in London, and our uninstructed pleasure in our puppy took fresh shape. Not for six months had we realized that the creature was a true poodle. Now, after three more months, we began to flatter ourselves that he might be a show poodle. Exactly what a show poodle was we did not know. But we felt it must be gratifying to have one.

7

*I*T MUST BE OBVIOUS ENOUGH, without my labouring the fact, that after nearly a year with Coco we were seraphically ignorant about dogs. We knew enough to take our puppy to the vet if he fell ill: scarcely more. If we wanted to teach him anything we simply told him what we wanted and left the rest to his good nature. As for the routine of his life, what he ate and when, how he spent the day and where he passed the night, he had settled that for himself. We interfered rarely, and then only if it was made clear to us that we must. For instance, when an expert at the barber's told us that Coco scratched himself because he ate too much sugar, we reviewed our dog's daily tea, wrung from a variety of indulgent sources, and decided that it included too many shortcake biscuits. No sweets, we said—only, of course, to flout our own edict. And yet we had convinced ourselves that we knew how to rear a puppy. And just as in the matter of dog-keeping we had swung from doubt to assurance, so in dog-fancying we jumped from disparagement to optimism. One day we had an old bundle of fur, possibly malformed; the next we began to have visions of Ch. Coco.

Not that we had any more knowledge of poodle points than on the day when we first saw a fawn puppy tumbling with his family in a back room in Campden Hill. I looked at L. E. Naylor's book *Poodles*, then looked at Coco. Did his lips show lippiness? I hoped not. Were his ribs well sprung and braced up? I had no idea. I looked at the illustrations. Was it, I asked myself, possible to mistake our pet for the lion-clipped beauty of the frontispiece, the cream Peaslake Hallmark? Hardly. Nor could I find much resemblance to the apricot Fircot Sunshine of Zizi Pom-Pom; but then Fircot Sunshine was a miniature and offered no fair comparison. We gave up the half-hearted attempt to master the jargon, and leaned back on our own aesthetic judgement. Coco, we said, looked all right to us. His coat was thick and soft, his carriage splendid: he had the figure of a Regency buck and the action of a Hackney pony. Our satisfaction was encouraged by the plaudits of others, and to their praise 'We think,' I replied, blushing, 'he's a good one'.

In the circumstances it was only natural that when any stranger came to call, whether it was a visitor from Hollywood or the man about the loose slate, our poodle should lollop downstairs at our heels to meet him and, if requested, solemnly shake hands. It was in this way that Coco secured an engagement on television.

Since then I have done a few days' work at Alexandra Palace and Lime Grove, but at the time I had only once been in a television programme, and it was with a mixture of apprehension and excitement that I signed a contract for half-an-hour on the last afternoon of August. It was a programme in a series devoted to the careers of a few women, professionals most of them in the arts; Joyce Grenfell, I remember, was among them. The plan was for an interviewer to elicit from each performer an account of her life, her work, her interests. There was to be no script. After all in television you cannot read from a script as you can in broadcasting, where your audience does not see you; but there would be several preliminary discussions. We began with two visits from a charming girl who listened with gratifying respect

FETCHING HIS COLLAR meant a morning walk; and a walk meant Doddie and Hyde Park, with leaps and bounds and pacific encounters with the regulars

to what I said, took notes, and produced a draft of the shape the interview might take. Next the resourceful interviewer sat at my table and looked at the chairs, the pictures and the ornaments on the chimney-piece. Last the producer himself, an old friend of mine from his days in radio, came to cast an eye over the subject at home.

From the start Coco was bound to be included. The series tried to present each woman in her natural setting, and the television service liked to borrow from her the means to reconstruct an authentic background: furniture, rugs, wall-decorations. The drafter, after marking down our Sunderland lustre pottery, made a note of the dog who, tired of blandishing, sprawled at my side: 'Can't we borrow Coco?' she said. At the next visit our poodle was there again, a silent, unobtrusive companion. By the time the producer S. E. Reynolds appeared, Coco's engagement was certain. He knew his part; it remained only to look to his wardrobe.

We felt it proper to add refinement to his dress at this moment: we had his feet clipped. The effect was to accentuate the luxuriance of his long, fringed cowboy trousers. From a distance he appeared to be standing on tiny castors; close to, his forepaws with their nails, their long fine bones and the pink skin showing through the shaven fur looked like an old lady's hands in beige silk gloves. His costume was attended to on the day before the performance; trimmed, clipped, bathed and combed, when the morning came he was eager, a dandy in cream, to jump into the BBC's station wagon and drive off to Alexandra Palace. I climbed in myself less insouciantly. For one thing I was not as confident of my reception as Coco was of his. For another I was uneasy about the plates, jugs, Greek bronzes and other oddments which I was carrying. The furniture had gone on ahead, but the minor fragments of décor rattled in a suitcase by my side. It was soothing to look down at my companion and find him calm, though a trifle inclined to bite his toenails.

The commissionaire examined us coldly as we scrambled out with our jugs and advanced to the inquiry desk. 'Is this dog a performer?' he asked. I had not thought of Coco as a member of a troupe, and for a moment I hesitated. 'No dogs allowed in the studio,' said the commissionaire, 'unless he's a performer'. I collected myself. 'Oh yes,' I said, 'he's going to perform all right'; and we bundled into the lift.

We reached the studio soon after ten in the morning. We did not leave until after four in the afternoon. Television, which adds to radio the business of set-dressing, make-up, lighting and a dozen other complications demanded by the camera, takes time and, from the point of view of the performer though not of the producer, wastes time; hours are spent waiting while cameramen and studio managers, electricians and carpenters, not to mention the other performers in the programme, work sweating amidst the hot lights and the cables. Yet the performer must be there on call; and Coco was ready.

For him there was none of the distraction of rehearsal and make-up. We all felt that with repetition his playing might grow stale. As for make-up, there was even a doubt lest in my enthusiasm I might already have overdone the beauty treatment. White is the impossible colour in television; turn the white page of a book, and the screen reflects a surrealist explosion. Coco, fresh from his bath, was so near white that somebody suggested a difficulty in recording his outline. It was a false alarm, and we settled down to the day's job. While I rehearsed I could see Coco sitting among the cables and the cameras. He showed no surprise at his surroundings. He trotted behind me when I went to the canteen for lunch, and accepted with a beaming smile the caresses of the waitresses. Only for half-an-hour, when somebody volunteered to put him on the lead and run him up and down the gardens, was he out of the hot, noisy building.

He came back joyfully. There is a mixture of informality and enthusiasm about a television studio which makes working there pleasant for the amateur. The technicians smile encouragingly, as if they wished with all their hearts that you might be a success. Coco found their company as congenial as I did, and by the time the lunch-hour was over and the performers were back, black-eyed and ochre-cheeked, from the make-up room, he had cemented a number of friendships. It was reassuring to see that he did not suffer from stage fright. But I was startled to discover how far his indifference to camera, lights, sound and action could go.

It had been decided that he should be called into the picture briefly, for though the English, as a foreigner has remarked, find it easier to talk to their dogs than to each other, interest in the performance of an untrained puppy readily flags. Coco, then, was urged, just before the studio fell silent, to wait quietly in the wings, and the programme began with Jeanne Heal tactfully leading me through an account of my life. Whether I was talking about travel in Greece or about the duties of a film critic I cannot recall. I remember only that I became suddenly aware of a sharp, melancholy whining. Its source was invisible to the television public, but to me it was only too clear. Coco was sitting on the floor out of camera range. He was hot, he was bored, he was tired of waiting for his cue; he was sick, too, of the sound of my voice, and he gave a great yawn, followed by a click of the teeth, to show it. After a moment or two his good manners reasserted themselves, and he fell silent again. But it was a relief to all of us when the chance came for him to show himself to his audience. That, he made clear, was all he wanted. He was called; he came forward with dignity and thrust his candid head into my hand; he allowed me to scratch him under the chin for a few seconds; then with an artist's timing he strolled away, lay down on the other side of the set, and was neither seen nor heard again.

'The perfect bit player,' said Leonard. 'He acted you all off the screen for thirty seconds.'

8

THIS WAS A TIME of unremitting self-advertisement for Coco. English pet-worship had brought several requests for permission to publish the broadcast on Cats and Dogs which had introduced him to an audience; and the appearance in print of my harmless ironies, the broadcast itself, and now Coco's own sally into the world of entertainment were too much for at any rate one correspondent, who sent me a quotation: 'It will be a happy day for England when Christian ladies transfer their affections from poodles and terriers to take care of destitute and starving children'.

His letter won my sympathy by its simple accents of exasperation. 'I once left a lodging,' he wrote, 'where my life was made a misery by a woman who idolized a dog she had. I tripped over it on the stairs, the dog watched me eat, shave and for all I know sleep as well. I was asked to watch it doing doggy tricks and listen to doggy talk, and sometimes had to indulge in this idiocy myself, for fear of being considered anti-dog'. As a matter of fact I had my own suspicions that Coco's début in television had received more attention that its modest range deserved. But my suspicions were not shared by Leonard or by Doddie. As for our dog's good looks, we grew every day more convinced that they were the sign of exceptional breeding.

Not that he cared. He took a fancy about that time to paddle. I repeat, to paddle: not to swim; he sensibly preferred to feel the ground under his feet. We believed that once he could be persuaded out of his depth he would enjoy swimming. But how could we persuade him? Only by example, or possibly force: swimming ourselves, we might coax him in, or we might carry him in and abandon him in a few feet of water. Selfishness triumphed over the duties of education. In the temperature of an English summer I too shrink from bathing, and we could hardly take our dog to the Riviera for swimming lessons. Coco continued to paddle: in duck-ponds, in country streams and, disregarding I fear the police notices, in the Serpentine. He went out for his morning walk in the Park a smart dog in cowboy chaps. He came back wet to the belly, his fur hanging in sooty rat's tails. If he was denied his paddle—and though it gave entertainment to the public we began to think that as law-abiders we ought to cut it short— he ran obstinately to the water-trough at the foot of the hill by the Hyde Park police-station, and sat in it. The water in the trough was not deep, but it was uncommonly dirty. That summer, indeed, layers of leaves, dust and bird-droppings had turned it to mud. Coco came home looking delighted with himself, and smelling like an old blanket used to stop a leak in the Paris drains.

I must not give the impression that he often mocked authority. But between him and Doddie, to whom he was devoted, there was a recognized system of tit-for-tat. If you deprive me of the match-box which I found in the waste-paper basket, his challenge would run, I shall take your gloves down-stairs and leave them on the floor. Very rarely he would break into erratic mischief. While I was at the Venice Film Festival, Leonard and Coco were invited to spend the week-end in the country. The gentle-men breakfasted in their dressing-gowns, and all were enjoying the bacon and eggs and the marmalade talk when someone looked out of the window and noticed that Coco, who like the rest had come down without his collar, was making a long barrow, or possibly a dyke, in the garden. He had chosen a spot in the middle of the beautiful and ancient lawn and was digging furiously; he had already gone deep enough to be hidden behind the earthworks he was throwing up. Whatever their gardener may have said, the hosts stifled all emotions harsher than curiosity. But everybody was puzzled. Our dog had never gone in for digging; show him a rabbit-hole, and he merely looked the other way. It was true that the sight and smell of a stretch of lawn or meadow now and then drove Coco into a frenzy of leaping, barking and galloping in circles. The momentary passion for excavation remained a mystery.

Such psychic disturbances were few; usually his society technique was unimpeachable. Once, I remember, I had foolishly brought together a visiting German archaeologist, a Philhellene acquaintance from the thirties, and Denys Hamson, author of *They Fell Among Greeks*, who had spent a fabulous year with the guerillas. I was unprepared for the difference in their memories of Greece, and my flurry of conviviality was not quick enough to smooth over the archaeologist's resentment when it turned out that his train had once been halted because Denys and party had blown up the bridge. Luckily Coco was there, and at this critical moment in international relations he rose blandly from under the table and offered to shake hands all round. To cynical minds, of course, it might have occurred that he was merely asking for a fried potato, a delicacy to which he was especially partial.

It was, then, under good auspices that Coco entered his second year. In the ten months which he had shared with us he had introduced a new light-heartedness into our preoccupied household. And I, who had so much feared an interruption of our comfortable programme, was bound to admit that he had merely strengthened the routine of the day. He had, as we had, his hours of silence and his hours of gossip, mornings when he was out of the house and evenings when letters must be taken to the post. And when the week-end broke the regularity of work-days he was a blonde shadow at our side: in the taxi, through the station, in the train, asking for no attention beyond the purchase of a dog-ticket, but persistently, indetachably there. So softly had he spun himself into our lives that I doubt whether at that time we realized our affection. About our vanity there was no doubt. We no longer made apologies for our dog. On the contrary: flushing, we defended him against even our own criticisms. His timidity, Leonard insisted, was a sign of intelligence. And when Josephine Blumenfeld hinted that his head was too big we indignantly denied it. Look, we said, pressing his ears back, it's all that fur; he's got a tiny head really. She was not convinced. How do you know, she asked, that he hasn't got some dreadful tropical disease? A week later she wrote from Paris: 'I think I have found some *Pommade pour la réduction des visages:* if I have, Coco shall have it as soon as I get back to England'.

Meanwhile we went on airily talking of exhibiting Coco. We joked about rushing him into the ring straight from the bath with his mutton-chop whiskers still clean. We enjoyed imaginary triumphs. But characteristically we did nothing. It was like buying a puppy all over again: we must do it, we said, we must—so often that we began to think it was done. Only this time Leonard never took action.

I do not remember what was the occasion when we saw the cream poodle in the train. We were travelling without Coco, I know, and we fell into conversation with the stranger's owner. The dog was leggy, with short rough curls all over, a square jaw, a black nose and dark eyes; a big creature, but not, apparently, big enough. 'He's just half an inch too short,' said the owner. 'I could have shown him otherwise, but he was ill as a puppy and he never grew to his proper size'. 'He looks,' we said politely in the vague respectful phrase, 'a good one'.

'Oh, yes,' she said, 'everything would be right if he were half an inch taller'.

'You know that dog . . .' I said thoughtfully in the taxi. 'Yes,' said Leonard, 'not a patch on Coco, was he?' 'His nose . . .' I said. 'Spoils him, that black nose,' said Leonard, 'and I don't care for those black eyes either; like squashed blackcurrants. The black looks all wrong'. 'Brown certainly is prettier', I agreed. We reminded one another how from the first we had been attracted by Coco's milk chocolate nose, and we drove home felicitating ourselves on the harmony achieved by brown nose and brown eye-circles in a cream-coloured face. We really ought to show him, we added.

And yet my satisfaction was gone. 'You know that dog,' I said again a few days later. 'The creature with the black nose?' said Leonard. 'You don't think . . .' I went on. 'Gives him a rather unpleasant expression . . .' said Leonard, 'the black makes him look much fiercer'. 'But the woman said everything was right except the size'. 'The black nose can't be right', said Leonard stubbornly.

We changed the subject, and for a time I forgot. But something stuck at the back of my mind. I found myself searching for the source of my uneasiness, and when I had tracked it down I found myself looking everywhere for cream-coloured poodles. The toy white bitch round the corner certainly had a black nose. But then white was not cream. I stopped strangers in the street and showed extravagant interest in their dogs, and once from the top of a bus I saw a poodle of exactly Coco's size and colour; but by the time I had come down the stairs he was gone, lost in the crowds at Marble Arch. Coco still drew the eyes of the anonymous public. Walking with him, we were conscious all the time of attentions ranging from the look, the cluck and the exclamation to the frank offer of endearment. But I wanted the approval of the expert.

One day I steeled myself to consult Naylor on noses. 'White puppies,' I read, 'must have black points—i.e. eyes, eye-rims, noses and lips'. So far, fair enough: Coco was not white. 'Apricots, if a dark

79

shade, may have brown points . . .' I looked at Coco, by now wearing his dingy November coat, and tried to convince myself that lamb-colour could be called dark apricot. 'But pale apricots, and also creams and silvers, must all have black points'. There it was at last in, as it were, black and cream. 'If you are seeking a show-quality puppy,' I read on, 'remember that pink points, or brown points on a cream or white, are a serious fault'. I recalled my first view of Coco: the brood in the outhouse, the splendid silver-blue mother, the many-coloured tumble of bodies and the little fawn animal breaking away from the scrum to scratch at my skirt. We had not been seeking a show-quality puppy. We had been looking for a brother to the astrakhan-covered, indiarubber creature we had seen going down the street one distant day in war-time. We had taken a year to realize it, but we had found much more than we had hoped. And for a moment we had fancied that we had indeed, without intention, found a show dog.

'I'm afraid,' I told Leonard, 'his nose is wrong. It ought to be black.'

'Black? With his pale colouring?'

I pointed to the authorities: not only his nose, but his eyes as well were inadmissible. 'I can hardly

believe it!' said Leonard. And once again I agreed:
'Brown certainly is prettier'. It was not until weeks
had passed, and the error of the nose had been con-
firmed from a variety of sources, that we could bring
ourselves to accept the colour-bar.

A few days later Coco fell dangerously ill. He
could have any nose he liked, or no nose at all, we
said miserably, if only he would be himself again.

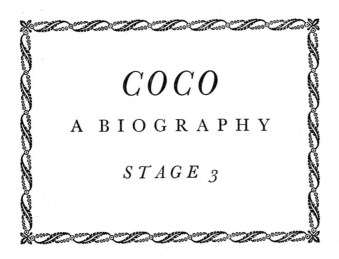

COCO

A BIOGRAPHY

STAGE 3

9

ONE EVENING we had noticed that he went to his rug beside the bed without insisting on the usual frolic first. We diagnosed a stomach demanding immobility after too much horsemeat too quickly shovelled in. When, next morning, he lay quiet at our first stir instead of bouncing to his feet we still were not disturbed. But when, after getting up, he sank down again with a apologetic air, when he sprawled by the breakfast table with his eyes closed and would not lift his head, we began to suspect something serious.

I had to go to Broadcasting House that day. 'I think,' I said to Leonard, 'it wouldn't do any harm if Doddie took him to the vet. Perhaps while she's there,' I added with elaborate casualness, 'she would ask if there's much hardpad about—just in case there are any precautions we ought to take, I mean'.

I went off to the BBC feeling anxious. Months

earlier the breeder of our dog had written to warn me about an epidemic of hardpad distemper in her district. Two of Coco's brothers had caught the disease, one was very ill. 'Don't bring Coco this way whatever you do.' About the same time I had happened on a newspaper article about hardpad. Preserving even in this my ignorance, I could not have recognized a single symptom. But I hurried Coco to the vet for hardpad inoculation (a different matter from distemper inoculation); and, having been discouraged by the news that £5 bought immunity for possibly a fortnight, continued to run him back for reassurance every time he so much as drooped a whisker.

I telephoned the house at lunch-time. 'No,' Leonard replied, 'the vet says it isn't hardpad'. 'But how is the dog?' The same, I was told; he's got a very high temperature and he's been given penicillin; the vet doesn't seem quite sure what's the matter with him. Late in the afternoon I went home to find Coco stretched limply in the study and everyone urging him in muted tones to cheer up. The vet, Doddie told me, suspected some grave infection: a kind of jaundice, she understood; penicillin he thought the best hope.

If we had not realized our affection before, we realized it fully now. It is easy for those who have never experienced the devotion of a pet creature to rise above sentimentality about animals, or indeed, like my exasperated correspondent, to adopt towards it a tone of moral reproof. But there is something inexpressibly sad in the look of a sick animal. A young animal in health lives at full pitch: enjoys to extremes, is always ready for anything. To see the splendid physical machine brought down to a crawl, the eyes uninterested, the spring in the muscles slack, is in itself heartrending. And the extinction of Coco's singular gaiety cast a shade over us all. One day he was a little engine of life in perpetual motion, thrusting his nose in our hands, pawing for attention, dancing with eagerness to go to the Park; the next he lay indifferently huddled like a pile of dead snow at a roadside.

When the following morning he went to the vet he was still lack-life; the penicillin injection must be repeated. I was, I said, not clear what was the matter. The vet replied, elucidating his first diagnosis, that he thought it might be leptospirosis, a kind of jaundice related to syphilis: a dangerous disease, often fatal and in any case likely if not at once scotched to become recurrent. Infectious, too; easily picked up by nosing some contaminated tree or tuft of grass; we ought to keep Coco away from other dogs. Unconsoled, I went home; Coco lay down again; and another day passed in dejection.

I am bound to admit that the period of illness was not long; it merely seemed long. One morning at our earliest stir Coco stirred too, got up, and tried for the first time for three days to wag his tail. Another day, and he was equal to sedate exercise; we almost applauded as he padded through the snow which lay early that year. Not that the danger was past. A week later there was another morning when Coco refused to get up for breakfast: more visits to the vet, more penicillin, more anxiety. It was weeks before we felt safe enough for Leonard to say, not without a certain hauteur, that our dog had recovered from an attack of syphilis.

We were not rid all through the winter of the fear of a relapse. And Coco's own carelessness about his health and diet did not help to reassure me. We spent Christmas with the Woodham-Smiths. While at Easter Leonard had fallen ill, this time I abused the best of hospitality by catching influenza (and giving it to our hosts). I was in no state to watch over a dog's dinner, and Coco took the opportunity to eat quantities of Christmas cake, turkey and plum pudding, not to mention a vast T-bone flown from New York which, elegantly wrapped, was handed him from the Christmas tree. Back in London, he looked first sorry, then ill—and I have never known anyone who could look more piteously ill. Presently he developed what we were told was gastric catarrh. He shook it off, but in the spring he had a second attack. This he used, I am afraid, to perfect his technique of regurgitating the pills which we flattered ourselves we had administered and laying them several minutes later on the study carpet.

Insecurity, however, merely strengthened our attachment to him. And now we had once entertained the fear that we might lose him we were delighted to see how anxious he was not to lose himself. Except in diet he was the most conservative creature alive; he tried nothing, not even once. That Christmas, before influenza had quite reduced me to apathy, I struggled out one afternoon. The roads were grooved with ice, under a guinea-hen sky the fields and banks gleamed sullenly white, and for anyone in spirits a country walk would have been magical. For anyone, that is, except Coco.

Leonard and I were boastful about his obedience in following at heel, and we liked to show how at the word of permission he would leap forward as if let off an invisible leash. So, when the main roads were safely passed and we took the frozen side-road, I gave the word. Run! I cried. Off you go! He plodded on at heel. Off you go! I repeated. Run, then! There was no response. I ran a few yards to encourage him. He ran too, but his nose remained obstinately pressed to the seam of my slacks. Walkies! I cried, desperately resorting to the jargon of the dog-nursery. He looked at me and tossed his head. I walked on. Never was there such following at heel; and little by little it dawned on me that in country which he did not know Coco preferred to stick to me. He would not leave my side until I turned towards home and he recognized territory already covered, when in a burst of bravado he picked up a knob of ice and ran off, challenging me to take it from him. Pride made him carry it—dropping it from time to time to puzzle over its temperature and diminishing size—until it had almost melted away in his mouth.

The qualities of caution and timorousness on which we now congratulated our dog had not ceased to fascinate the Emperor. Soundless as smoke he ran up and down stairs behind us. When we went into the garden he stalked us from behind a screen of shrubs; and once in a bid for Coco's attention he brought a dead bird into the house and gave a dazzling exhibition of single-handed badminton. We could not fail to admire the marks of his Siamese breeding: the narrow skull, the sharp ears, the exquisite dark points; and it is possible that we reflected a little mournfully on Coco's nose. But the disappointment no longer really distressed us. We had the dog back alive; in our gratitude we were glad to overlook any trifling errors in pigmentation. In any case he was to our eyes still incomparably handsome. The experts might like black noses. We liked brown noses, we said; and when strangers asked, as they often did, whether we had shown him, we remembered the owner of the cream poodle in the train and replied that we were prevented by one little detail; everything else was perfect. And so indeed it seemed to us as we looked out of the window of the waiting night ferry train at Victoria one February evening. We were on our way to a week's holiday in Barbizon. Doddie was taking Coco to supper with her mother, and as he came down the next platform with ears gently flapping, bouncing on his indiarubber pads and flinging his feet up, we nudged one another: 'Are you sure there's no chance of showing him?' said Leonard.

All the same it was a shaggy bundle of poodleskin that greeted us when we came home again.

10

IN THE WINTRY WEATHER we did not have Coco trimmed often or closely, and his wool, rapidly growing, lost the grotesque and beautiful contours drawn by the clippers of the Dog Bath Shop. By the beginning of the spring, with his stained whiskers, stringy trousers and overgrown coat, he hardly looked a poodle at all, and his nose, criminal though it was, could scarcely injure his appearance.

It was just as well that his illness had reconciled us to his first lapse from the rules, for there was more to come. As a cream poodle he had, we knew now, points of the wrong colour. But he had begun life with a coat of fawn-coloured silk. Leonard began to insist that we had not a cream but an apricot poodle. I pointed to the gradual paling of Coco's fur since he had come to live with us. It was well known, I said grandly, that poodles, unlike Siamese cats, with age grew lighter in colour, not darker:

Coco's mother herself had turned from black to the shade called in the poodle world blue. In vain. Look, said Leonard, his ears are quite dark; and look at his muzzle, you can see it's going ginger. I remonstrated: it's the dog growing lighter, not the muzzle growing darker. Mark my words, said Leonard with mock emphasis, in six months' time that dog will be apricot, and his brown nose will match. And, he added, it may be our *duty* to show him and give the poodle-fanciers a treat.

Looking back, I have to admit that there was truth in the contention that Coco was growing darker. He was growing darker because he was getting dirtier. His untrimmed coat soaked up greasy soot from the grass in the Park, and the muffs of fur which overhung his shaven feet were the tone of lead. Under Leonard's influence I sometimes brazened it out, and to the question, What colour do you call that? I answered boldly: Apricot. But one day my bluff was called—by Richard Massingham, who I am sure knows everything about dogs; at any rate he owns two handsome poodles of his own. It can have been nothing but courtesy which made him ask, not indeed: What colour do you call that? but: What colour is that? So polite was the question that it answered itself, and as I opened my mouth to say 'Apricot', Richard Massingham on the very instant brought out the word 'Cream'. And as I began to retract, he began to apologize. But by then I had once and for all renounced the pretence that Coco was anything but a cream poodle with the wrong nose. And, as it now appeared, truancies of shade too. It was a fact that his muzzle was ginger and that his ears were a pale apricot. A few ginger hairs grew among the cream on his hocks and his spine as well, but they had no business there. He should have been all one colour: a solid colour, as the breeders say. Even his ears were a mistake.

At eighteen months he could no longer be called, in my sentimental phrase, only a puppy, and I was persuaded that he had reached his proper size. Leonard, however, maintained that Coco would grow taller. He was right. In his third winter our dog could no longer sit without stooping under the table in the bizarre upright position which he had previously sustained while trying to entice a piece of bacon to jump off a plate into his mouth. But the second spring found him undeveloped in matters other than size. I once asked, ignorantly confident of approval, if we were not right to mix a few green vegetables with his dinner. Nonsense, said the vet, an old-fangled type whom I then patronized, he'll provide himself with green vegetables by eating grass. I protested that he never ate grass. He will, said the vet, you'll see. But he never did. Never, that is, unless I picked it for him, when he would snatch a blade or two from my hand and chew it impatiently. Nature had not told him about eating grass. For a long time we thought Nature had forgotten to mention the proper bearing of a manly dog at a lamp post. When, very late, he mastered the technique of the standing instead of the sitting method, he contrived on three legs to look like a prentice ballerina maintaining bravely but insecurely a difficult pose on one. At the age of two he still puzzled when his acquaintances in the Park indulged in the traditional stamp-and-scratch. It was only rarely that, looking round in a deprecatory way, he gave a tentative flip of his back paws.

The fact is that he was not growing into a manly dog. Our friends had manly dogs: dogs who fought, dogs who bit the postman. Freda Bruce-Lockhart, after bringing up a litter of bull-terriers, told me that as puppies two of them had to be kept in separate rooms; left together, they would have torn off one another's ears. Coco fought with nobody. Once or twice Doddie came back from the Park with a report that he had growled when another dog made insulting proposals. We were inclined, I am afraid, to say that Doddie's hearing was sharpened by affection. In my experience at any rate whenever an accoster made the opening gambit of the grab at the back of the neck, our Ferdinand tucked in as much of himself as he could, burst out of the mêlée, and ran. The only living creatures he ever defied were ourselves— and then only in play. He would take a packet of cigarettes off the table and bore tooth-holes through the cardboard and the cigarettes inside, snatch the handkerchief from Leonard's breast-pocket, or seize Leonard's hat from a chair. When he had worked the band off the old hat he began dismantling the new one, and he was once discovered mumbling over a hat of Doddie's. I looked on these excesses with a disapproval which turned to bad temper when the thing purloined was found to be my hat. But Coco refused to be intimidated. Growling, he danced away with his prize, and when he was scolded into giving it back the sounds of his mock fury were blood-curdling.

These innocent games may seem to accord ill with the nature of a dog who in his second year could boast an attack of leptospirosis. Perhaps this is the place to say that we came in the end to discredit Coco's dangerous malady. Not until much later: all that winter, as I have said, we watched him rather nervously, and even when we began to dismiss the danger of a relapse there was still the fear that he might have been left with some permanent weakness. A damaged kidney, we were told, was a likely consequence. But time went by; Coco was as gay as a grasshopper; until one day months afterwards he caught a cold in one of his wrong-coloured eyes. I took him to the vet. An authoritative young man, partner in an establishment which I had not visited before, attended to him, and I took the opportunity of airing my fears. No, said the vet, his kidneys seemed all right; and what made me think they were anything else?

The medical profession is entitled to its differences of opinion. It is not for me to take sides. But I came away with a doubt in my mind. Perhaps Coco's alarming illness had not been leptospirosis after all. We began to wonder if he had ever so much as had tonsillitis.

And we continued to wonder if he had the far-seeing eyes with which the poodle is credited. Doubts revived when, coming upstairs from the surgery to the waiting-room, he blundered into a wall. Have you noticed anything wrong with his sight? asked the vet, but could not himself find a visible defect. 'He sees with his nose', said Leonard. All the same when Coco in the Park gave an enthusiastic leap and set off at a gallop towards a car, I fancy he was seeing with his eyes. He was merely mistaking a very large motor in the far distance for a very small dog close at hand.

His interests had changed since the days when he was ready to run with all comers. Perhaps it is true that living with human beings corrupts an animal. Certainly his existence in our household was a mimicry of our own: the same meal-times, the same week-ends, the same descents into inertia. He came to prefer our company to the company of his own kind. At the sight of a fair-sized dog he sometimes ran to the encounter, sometimes took up the doggy attitude: stopped dead, bristling slightly, then advanced slowly with carefully controlled movements, picking his feet up and laying them stealthily down again; yet when he came nose to nose with the stranger he turned away indifferently. Frequently he did not even bother with the ritual of advance and withdrawal and kept at our heels to avoid trouble, and the miniature poodles to whom he had as a puppy shown such gallantry now gambolled round him in vain. He doesn't want to play with dogs any more, we said sadly.

It had not escaped us that he might have other ideas; a young animal frisking through a second spring begins eyeing the girls. Some acquaintance or other would offer us sympathy: 'Such a nuisance, the way a dog will run off; I've always had bitches. So much more affectionate, and more your own dog, if you know what I mean'. She would have doubted it, but we did not know what she meant: impossible to be more affectionate than Coco. All the same we were ready to find some day that another kind of love had distracted him.

And yet the months passed without disturbing his calm. Of course he was aware of a strange, fresh interest in life: ran to look out of the window, trotted down the street behind an unresponsive bitch. 'These poodles are all so sexy', cried one woman in out-raged tones when our dog made modest and mistaken advances to a very young, very small Pekinese on a leash. But in truth poor Coco had little chance to learn the niceties. Londoners keep their pets in purdah during the season for love, or at best take them out under guard, and except for an unsatisfactory romp in a country lane with a black spaniel coyer than Marvell's Mistress his education was at a standstill—though at the farm a tortoiseshell cat, I am sorry to say, did what she could, climbing in through the window, flinging herself at his knees, and uttering rippling cries of endearment which left him puzzled but cold. We could hardly blame him if in his unnatural segregation he formed unconventional attachments. Once at a restaurant in France, long before our dog-days, I had ventured to ask the diamond-cut Frenchwoman at the next table the breed of her magnificent attendant. 'C'est un Boxair, Madame', she said frigidly, dragging the creature away. Coco in the spring entertained romantic feelings towards a variety of dogs; our French encounter enabled us to put a name to his favourites. He found Boxers irresistible.

The wrong nose, eyes, and lips; a coat with unpardonable variations of colour; a nature unmanly to the point of effeminacy—there was not much left of our high social ambitions. One more blow was to fall.

The first summer, on a Saturday afternoon when his coat was freshly trimmed, we took him to the village fête. The grounds of Hever Castle, once Ann Boleyn's home, were open for the occasion: children squeaked in the maze, visitors wandered by the moat and along the alleys by the exiled Mediterranean statuary, and amidst applause Coco ran barking in circles on the emerald plush lawns. By the lake we stopped for the view. Leonard and I leaned on the stone balustrade, and the dog drank loudly where the water lapped at the terrace. There was a splash. Coco had fallen into the lake. His topknot was held high in the manner of inexperienced bathers, and his face wore a look of mild indignation.

Swim! we commanded, swim! But already he had scrambled ashore; his ears dripped, wet fur clung to his legs and ribs, and beneath it he was a skinny little whippet, a model for an anti-vivisection poster. Everybody laughed as we walked back, and we could not help thinking ourselves that his head seemed too big.

We were reminded of this in the winter when the country mud caked on his trousers and gave him a topheavy look. In the spring we took to washing him ourselves now and then. After the bath in an outhouse at the farm we towelled him till he grunted, then ran with him up and down the road; as he dried I sat by the fire and combed him into a shape which was pleasing but not poodleish. Again we gazed at his head. It was sadly unlike the head of any of the poodles in the books or even the newspapers. The muzzle looked short and broad, the skull wide. 'I believe,' I said, 'Josephine Blumenfeld was right: his head *is* too big'. And this time Leonard agreed. 'His head is wrong, his nose is wrong, his ears are wrong—everything,' he said mournfully, 'is wrong'. Our Ugly Duckling, it seemed, was not a swan after all.

I I

DUCKLING OR SWAN, he was part of our lives. I suppose it is inevitable that human beings should attribute to their pets the power of human speech. We were not innocent of the folly, but instead of putting infant phrases into the mouth of our dog, we found ourselves taking it for granted that we all three should understand one another. It never struck us that he was, I will not say dumb but silent. We felt that he talked just as much as we did.

I do not mean only that he yelped in his sleep or groaned if he was kept waiting for his dinner. I mean that he managed to be conversational without making a sound. Perry had done much the same. Not that he was soundless: far from it. His Siamese voice would be heard hourly, asking angrily for a door to be opened, or simply demanding, hang it all, a bit of attention. But when he fell taciturn he was equally successful in telling us what he wanted. The look on his back as he sat facing the anthracite stove, now and then edging half-an-inch closer until his nose almost touched the mica, was enough to make me turn the heat up. Coco's most telling remarks, too, were silent. But where Perry had been imperious Coco was plaintive. When, grouped round the fire at the farm after his home shampoo, we at last stopped towelling him, he lay quiet for a minute, then began to shiver. We took up the towel and he stopped shivering; we laid it down, and his expression said clearly that he might not be long for this world.

As he grew his gentle demands on our affection increased. Sensual as a cat, he liked to be scratched on the chin, behind the ears, on the chest. He would appear beside one's chair, look searchingly into one's face, lay a paw on one's knee. His persistence was irresistible, and we obliged him by the hour; Leonard, who had begun by pooh-poohing, became the most tireless scratcher of us all. Coco made us change our tune about other matters too. During the first months of our acquaintance we had doubted him absurdly. Because he could not at once jump we had supposed that he would never jump. When blinking he let the biscuit we threw fall on his nose we assumed that he would never catch. By the time he was two we had come to boast of his agility and his adroitness.

Advanced dog-owners nowadays send their dogs to be professionally trained in obedience. In America, I gather, they join their pets in class and learn to make themselves obeyed. Leonard and I remained deplorably ignorant of the principles of command. We had heard about forcing the dog with a choke-collar to do what he is told. We had read about the famous American poodle-trainer who recommends throwing a piece of chain at the animal to stop him barking when the bell rings, firing a gun to keep him quiet at night, or discouraging him from sitting on the sofa by putting a mouse-trap on it. Our method was innocent of collars, chains, guns and traps. Or rather we got along without any method. Looking back, we cannot help thinking that few dogs would have been as easy to teach.

Leonard taught him to catch. At first Coco found it difficult to get the hang of playing forward or, as the case might be, back to the paper ball. But soon he learned to judge distance. Instead of standing fatalistically waiting for the ball to land on his head he backed away or jumped forward and upward.

For the easy missile Leonard substituted an empty twenty-cigarette Du Maurier box. Coco caught the awkward thing and stood drooping his head and turning his eyes up so that the whites showed in horizontal crescents, giving him an expression at once naughty and braggart. The box sometimes turned in the air; he caught it by its width and held it with his jaws extended to accommodate its four inches. 'With that mouth he could carry a pheasant', said Leonard, and threw two cigarette-boxes together. Coco caught them, as he caught the magazines rolled for the post which, amidst my protests of 'Too Heavy', were half-thrown, half-dropped into his mouth. Presently he could catch three empty cigarette-packets at once; then Leonard worked him up to four. Growing ambitious, we tried to teach him to balance a biscuit on his nose, then toss it up and catch it. At about the sixth attempt he understood what we wanted him to do and did it. We substituted an empty cigarette-box. Four or five tries, and Coco had learned to tilt his muzzle and flick the cardboard into his mouth.

But impatience on our part nearly wrecked his career as an athlete. Once he had mastered the elements of jumping—once, that is, he had learned to jump on to the bed—we began to think of more advanced exercises. A poodle is by tradition an acrobat, and we noticed how prettily our dog would clear some country obstacle, say a ditch in a meadow. With morsels of biscuit we lured him over the bottom half of the stile by the white mare's pasture, or we stood in the garden, held a stick for a bar, and waved a handkerchief, a trophy he always coveted, on the other side. The take-off was the difficulty. No high jumpers ourselves, we felt all the same that we knew something about the business, and first among our convictions was that a run-up was a help. Coco did not believe in the run-up. If we insisted, of course, he would advance bouncing, but when he came to the bar he would stop dead, then jump from a standing position. His achievement was erratic, but at his best he seemed to us to jump like a flea. We borrowed a hoop from the children at the farm and invited him to try it. He took fire at our cries and sprang through it and back again, sneezing with excitement.

At this stage we got above ourselves. Dusky, the young Alsatian who had won our hearts, had thought nothing of clearing a five-barred gate. Even Dawn, though she was no jumper, was ready for a shot; she once gamely followed her daughter over the farm gate, with the result, I am bound to admit, that after an awkward scrabble on the top bar she fell flat on her face. Naturally we did not expect Coco to perform such prodigies. But that he was physically able to jump three feet or more we were certain, and one day on our week-end walk we saw a chance to test him. A gate into a meadow had broken from its hinges and half-lay at an angle to the slope of the ground: not a simple jump perhaps, but not a big one either, and we had seen Coco manage a greater height. We invited him into the field. He flew over; we cheered and he joined in the applause. 'Back again!' we called. 'Over!' As he hesitated we added professionally 'Hup!' He barked, gathered himself, pranced forward and jumped. He cleared the gate. But as he came down on the near side one of his hind legs caught between a crossbar and the diagonal, and with alarm we saw him hanging head down. When we lifted him off he shrieked, and for the next five minutes his cries must have been heard a mile away. His paw was not damaged. After lengthy endearments he consented to hobble away with us; presently the limp vanished and he was scampering as usual. But we had had a fright, and it was some time before we suggested jumping again.

We need not have worried about the risk. He would jump through a hoop with pleasure, but at the offer of a gate he looked the other way, and once when I tried brutal measures and, leaving him outside, walked away across a field, he merely sat in the lane and yelled. I came back, defeated, to find him on terms of warm friendship with a one-armed tramp whose sympathy he had won during my absence.

All the same when he was two and a half Coco never failed in reasonable obedience. He followed impeccably at heel, stopped dead when his companion stopped, moved on when his companion moved. Even when catching a train Leonard and I never found it necessary to lead him, and he would hurry unattached across Victoria Station behind us, dodging through the crowds as if drawn by a magnet. If on a walk one of us said to him Stay! no matter how casually the syllable was spoken he stood stock still, waiting while we went across the road or round a corner and out of sight. He would not move until we called him.

At a word he would sit, lie down or stand up, and at the command Drop! he would stop in mid-gallop and couch in his tracks; to gesture him to drop was almost enough. Or he could be directed to go to one or the other of us: skim upstairs, for instance, to the bedroom where Leonard was changing. He doted on Leonard. The rest of us he greeted with warmth, and Doddie in particular he loved, but at the appearance of the man of the family his enthusiasm was uncontrollable. I sometimes took him for a walk while Leonard played golf. As we came back he bristled with excitement at the thought of reunion, and it was all he could do to wait; at last when we were about two hundred yards from the golfer, 'There he is!' I said, and Coco rushed off, frequently in the wrong direction but always in a rapture.

Most dogs, I suppose, can be taught an elementary form of carrying, some can be taught fetching as well. I remember how dashed I was when, after I had been boasting about Coco to a hospitable dog-owner in Birmingham, she put down her glass and said quietly to her mongrel: 'Go upstairs and fetch Mum's spectacles!' and sure enough he fetched them. Coco soon learned to carry. He ran to the kitchen carrying the parcel of grass which we brought from the country for our vegetable-starved cat. Ennis sent him in with the letters, and we employed him as a runner to take papers or books from one member of the family to another.

But we were not at first particularly successful in teaching him to fetch. He made a great show of retrieving the stick we threw in the stream, but more often than not he came out carrying a bit of straw or a twig or, with an expression which said clearly that he was not to blame, nothing at all. Then Doddie had the idea of teaching him to fetch his new collar, a gentlemanly accoutrement of sober brown leather with brass studs which had replaced the gaudy red of youth. A collar to him meant going out for a walk. 'Fetch your collar!'—he bustled off and brought it with alacrity. We were enchanted, one day when his outing was delayed, to see him waiting unasked with the symbol in his mouth.

One evening at a pub in Thame the barman, looking at our dog, who was freshly spruced, asked: 'Is he a good performer?' Oh yes, said Leonard vaguely, not at first taking the man's meaning. A minute later we realized with pride that we had been put down as a music-hall turn. Emphatically we repeated to one another that Coco was indeed a good performer; there was nothing he could not be taught to do. Were he rightly trained, we said, he might earn a living for us all. Then we had a moment's doubt. Some things he could not be taught to do. He was not slavish. He would jump over a branch, but not over Leonard's shooting-stick, to which he had taken a dislike. He would carry a book, but not his lead. His patience during instruction suddenly gave out and he would sit back with a loud click of his jaws; once he had clicked there was no persuading him. This obstinacy or, as we preferred to call it, this independence of character might stand in the way of a great career in the circus ring.

We liked him the better for it. Though we could no longer pretend that he was poodle-perfect, we now believed that we had discovered a nonpareil of intelligence. Accidentally discovered: we could take no credit to ourselves; the choice of our puppy had been chancy, his rearing haphazard and his education casual. Everything in his life seemed to happen by accident, and by accident it was that when he was about two the style of his barbering was changed. He had always worn moustache and beard, and the water he drank dripped from his whiskers to the first lap on which he laid his chin. We asked for a beard trim. The hairdresser took us at more than our word, and when Coco came home he was clean-shaven.

For an hour or two we were appalled, for a day or two we could not accustom our eyes to the long, refined nose which had taken the place of the whiskered muzzle. But soon we accepted the change with delight. To balance the smooth chin his top-knot had been cut narrow, and long ears flowed out from beneath the crown of a furry cream bowler; the effect was that of a pinhead exquisite. After all, we said triumphantly, his head isn't too big. Our spirits, always buoyant where Coco was concerned, bobbed up once more.

COCO

A BIOGRAPHY

FINALE

THIS STORY has been written at close range. But though it begins with infancy, it does not end with old age. I have a death to tell: not our dog's; Coco has, we hope, his life ahead of him. Smut it was who died young and mourned, leaving Coco without his golden-eyed rival.

The two had little parley the last year or so. The cat chose to be cherished in the kitchen by Nancy and Ennis, and favoured the rest of the house with only occasional visits. Coco lives (for now I can speak of the present) at Leonard's elbow, at Doddie's and mine, and visits the kitchen at fixed hours only. He has a rigid time-table. The man of the house goes down to breakfast first. Coco waits for me, then snatches his collar and runs to the study in time for a morsel of egg and bacon or whatever is going. After breakfast he waits at the top of the stairs until Doddie comes to take him for a walk. In the afternoon he is out again, and at tea-time is taken to the Post Office, where he has friends who keep a bag of biscuits. On his return he rushes the evening papers to the kitchen, where Nancy and Ennis offer him another biscuit. He listens, his nose through the banisters, for Leonard's taxi, gives passionate welcome, and dines with the two of us. At midnight he trots round the block again. In the bedroom he insists that Leonard shall scratch him for a few minutes before, contented, he sprawls on his rug for the night.

We are not besotted enough to suppose that nobody laughs at our attachment to our dog. We laugh at it ourselves. But everyone tolerates it. Of course there have been times when he was left behind. Dog-owners are sometimes reluctant to ask him to their houses; and I remember Olive Cook and Edwin Smith inviting us to dine without him—an understandable arrangement, since Edwin's cat was in accouchement in a cardboard box under the sitting-room table. 'Clever girl!' Olive encouraged the mother as each new-born mew was heard. But as a rule Coco has come with us everywhere: to the family party with my brother Ivor and his wife Freda; to the week-end with the Master of the Pytchley; to tea in Acacia Road at my old friend S. S. Koteliansky's house, where he accepted a cream cracker and slept through the talk about D. H. Lawrence. He always gives the impression of enjoying himself. Yet with another spring we begin to wonder if human companionship is enough. He has recovered his interest